Elvis in Texas

The Undiscovered King 1954-1958

Lori Torrance
with
Stanley Oberst

Republic of Texas Press

Republic of Texas Press is an imprint of Wordware Publishing, Inc.

Distributed by NATIONAL BOOK NETWORK

ISBN: 978-1-55622-887-2

Contents

To my sister, Shari, for her unending patience with "the project";

To my mother, who promptly whipped out her collection of 45s and started a nostalgia fest;

To my father, whose cryptic admission, "I don't remember the fifties, I was in the army," even made the waiter laugh (I guess you had to be there);

And especially to Ginnie Bivona and the DFW Writer's Workshop for all the opportunities, moral support, and unwavering friendship through the worstest and bestest of times.

Introduction

Long before he dreamed of pink Cadillacs and paparazzi, a musical wannabe named Elvis Presley and his two faithful sidekicks tore up Texas highways, perpetually late for their next high school hop, car dealership opening, or Lion's Club fund raiser. As they dodged tumbleweeds at 110 mph to play at every wide spot in the road, scores of abused cars and unwary rattlesnakes sacrificed their lives so that one day Elvis Presley could tell a Dallas newspaper reporter, "I owe a lot to Texas. They're the ones who put me over the top."

Though to most good ol' boys (and gals) Elvis was a mystery wrapped in a riddle inside a pink and black suit, anyone who met him knew he possessed that certain something. No matter what the folks in Texas thought of his creative wardrobe, dubious bodily exertions, or guitar homicide, all agreed Elvis served as an excellent musical ambassador. They just weren't sure from what planet.

These are their stories....

Courtesy of Polly Webb

Well, it's a one for the money . . .

The Once and Future King

October 2, 1954 - Nashville - The Grand Ole Opry

The free calendars at the farm bureau read 1954. On the counter a freshly printed copy of *Lord of the Flies* lay next to a bottle of Grapette, a handful of peanuts backstroking through the purple fizz. Country music twanged on the radio, Hank Williams crying in his cornflakes again. Every so often a station break reminded you of its call letters, broadcasted the Supreme Court's recent verdict in the public school desegregation case, or repeated Edward R. Murrow's denunciation of Senator Joseph R. McCarthy as a communist witch hunter.

Meanwhile, Jimmy Stewart stared through the *Rear Window* of his apartment, wondering what was in the trunk and where his neighbor's wife suddenly disappeared to, Lucy Ricardo and Ethel Mertz climbed the ledge of their brownstone dressed as Martians, and the Grand Ole Opry gave Elvis Presley the Grand Ole boot.

On July 10, 1954, five days after it was recorded, the young unknown's radical rendition of "That's Alright, Mama" spun on Dewey Phillips' WHBQ "Red, Hot and Blue" turntable in Memphis. The switchboard lit up like a firestorm. Who was that guy?

Dewey and record producer Sam Phillips dragged the soft-spoken teenager into the studio to interview him on the air and satisfy listener curiosity. Elvis skittered over to a chair in the recording booth and perched like a man holding a one-way ticket on the *Titanic*. Dewey took one look at the quivering introvert sitting across from him and lied like a rug. Hey, I've got a few records cued, so let's just gab for a few minutes, Dewey told Elvis. I'll tell you when we're ready to start. The young man nodded nervously.

Remember when...

you had to wait for your neighbors to get off the party line before you could make your phone call? With six other households sharing your line, you might never get a chance to make that all-important call, unless your neighbors hung up so they could eavesdrop on your conversation. Three rings ... that's your house, I believe.

So, what school d'ya go to? Dewey asked him innocently enough. It seemed the listening audience loved the tune, but couldn't tell what color the singer was.

Humes High, Elvis told him. (Bingo, he's white.)

That apparently urgent matter clarified, the two shot the breeze for a few more minutes. Finally Dewey said, Alright Elvis, thank you very much. The teenager did a double take. Aren't you gonna interview me?

I already have, Dewey told him. The mike's been open the whole time.

Elvis melted into a horrified puddle on the seat.

The next couple of nights, Elvis returned to Sun Records studio to come up with a B-side ditty for "That's Alright, Mama." The audience had spoken; they wanted that song and they wanted it yesterday, or the day before if at all possible. Record stores begged Sun for the single. Sam Phillips arranged Scotty Moore and Bill Black from the Starlite Wranglers to play backup, just as he did for the first recording session. Elvis, Scotty, and Bill had already broken the ice musically the last time they met, so they rolled out a revved version of "Blue Moon of Kentucky" in short order. By July 19, six thousand advance orders awaited the delivery truck.

A bit overwhelmed by the attention, Elvis asked the older and hopefully wiser

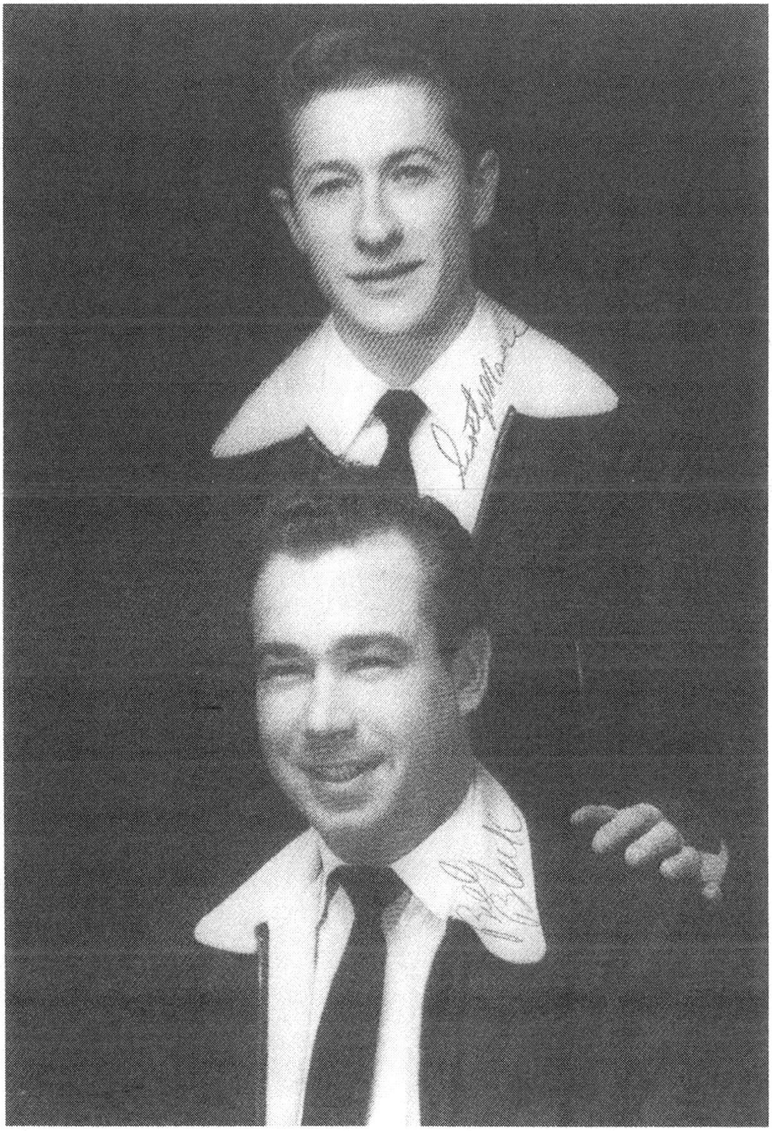

Blue Moon Boys, Scotty Moore and Bill Black. Courtesy of Elsie Medlin

Don't quit your day job. The Opry's suggestion to Elvis must surely go down in history as the worst career advice since scouts told Custer that Little Big Horn sounded like a swell career-advancing move.

Scotty Moore to act as his temporary manager. Scotty got 10 percent off the top for his pains and 25 percent of the split. Meanwhile, the boys earned their daily biscuit: Elvis as a Crown Electric truck driver, Bill at Firestone, and Scotty at his brother's dry cleaning business.

Sam Phillips decided Elvis and the Blue Moon Boys (as they now called themselves) needed to play the Grand Ole Opry for exposure. Sam managed to convince the Opry's booking agent, Jim Denny, to slide them into any loose chink in the bill. On October 2 Elvis, Scotty, Bill, the Blue Moon Boys' better halves, and Sam Phillips piled into Sam's black Cadillac (the wheels of choice in the south) and caravanned to Nashville.

Hoping to provoke a tear or two, Elvis decided to sing "Old Shep" to the staunchly country Opry audience. But the institution's rules read that singers could only perform what they officially recorded for the label. That gave them a whopping choice of three: "That's Alright, Mama," "Blue Moon of Kentucky," and their newborn of a couple of days, "Good Rockin' Tonight."

Elvis quavered through both side A and B of the 45; the conservative collective remained unimpressed. He wilted offstage as the murmur of disapproval followed him. That didn't sound like country to me, no sir. I tell you, Ethel, I know country when I hear it and I ain't heard it. No sir. This show is going to Purgatory in a pouch.

Backstage, Jim Denny suggested to Elvis that the boy had a real future in truck driving . . . stick to it. The Cadillac drove the two hundred miles back to Memphis in silence. The people inside didn't talk either.

Hayride to the Rescue

October 16, 1954 - Shreveport - Louisiana Hayride

Briiiiing, briiiiiing.

Sun Studios, may I help you?

This is Tillman Franks of the Louisiana Hayride. I'm looking for one of your artists, a Mr. Elvis Presley. Is he there?

I'm sorry, Mr. Franks, he isn't here today.

Okay, I'll try back later.

Briiiiing, briiiiiing.

Sun Studios, may I help you?

Yeah, this is Tillman Franks of the Louisiana Hayride again. I'm still looking for Elvis Presley. Is he in yet?

I'm sorry, Mr. Franks, he hasn't come in today. May I take a message?

Yes, tell him to get a pager.

A what?

Never mind, I'll call back later.

A couple days later Tillman reached Elvis Presley, almost too late to do either of them any good. Opportunity was knocking, but Elvis stared through the peephole in his pajamas.

Tillman explained that he booked the Louisiana Hayride in Shreveport as well as played in the band. One of his acts, Jimmy and Johnny, had a gig in New Mexico in which Tillman agreed to play backup on bass. But Horace Logan, emcee of the Hayride, told Tillman he needed him that weekend. Tillman had begun preliminary negotiations. If he could find a ~~victim~~ replacement, it was Lousiana in his rearview mirror. And he knew just the singer.

Okay, so the Opry hated the kid. But they hated anything that smelled like it might have a drumbeat. Tillman's DJ friend Tommy Cutner played Elvis's record on the air so often the needle had almost dug to China. Lo mein sprung from the grooves on each revolution.

Who knows, maybe the younger and hipper crowd of the Hayride would get a kick out of the mutilated version of "Blue Moon" and its singer. Stranger things had happened.

So, how about it, kid? Wanna play the Hayride?

Sure. When?

Tomorrow.

Gulp.

The next afternoon Elvis, Scotty, and Bill rolled into the parking lot of the Hayride and did yoga breathing exercises. Inside, lay the Hank Williams holy shrine, ground zero for country music worshippers.

Tillman and Horace Logan greeted Elvis, Scotty, and Bill with the warmth of invited guests. Tillman told the boys they'd play in the first segment, where all the fresh new talent got broken in. While they waited their turn, Elvis occupied himself by meeting the other singers backstage. The family atmosphere seemed to calm him, until Horace Logan announced them.

What a difference a day makes. E. at the Hayride, 1955. Courtesy of Bobby Holeman

Once again, Elvis sidestepped nervously onto the stage. The audience wanted to like him, they really did, but he sang like he was stapled to a pole. They applauded generously anyway, and the threesome retreated behind stage to resuscitate their hearts.

You don't get the reputation for new talent by overlooking unpolished diamonds, and Horace Logan and Tillman Franks thought they saw a sparkle behind the rigid frame. Tillman took Elvis aside and told him that he and Horace decided to let them play again in the second segment. Relax a little, Tillman told the singer. Just go out there and do your thing.

Throwing caution to the wind, Elvis returned to the stage. This time his leg started moving. His voice caught hold and he rocked to the beat. Suddenly, his hip jerked to the side. A collective squeal pealed out of the female contingency. Fired up by their response, he dropped all pretenses of shyness and grooved through the rest of his set. Their

This isn't so hard! E. and the boys at the Hayride, 1955. Courtesy of Pat Green

last chord struck a chord with the onlookers. They screamed and applauded, jumping up and down.

Horace moved in swiftly, cornering them barely ten feet off the stage. How about a year contract, he asked them. They looked at each other. Well, alrighty then. It's a deal.

Elvis, Scotty, and Bill re-met Tillman before they left that night. Thank you, Mr. Franks, for the opportunity, Elvis told him.

In three short months, Elvis would pole vault over the ranks and headline the show. The nervous young man on stage dissipated that night, replaced by a provocative he-siren who lured girls with his come-hither voice. Elvis might not have completely understood why his performances caused such a meltdown of moral certainty, but he certainly learned how to capitalize on it in short order. A few months from this night, Horace Logan would tell Elvis that his phrasing was too suggestive for a G-rated audience. I don't try to sing them suggestively, Elvis protested. The girls didn't complain, however.

Meanwhile, Tillman Franks pondered the possibilities for this young man in front of an audience of wild Texas women. Thank *you*, Mr. Presley . . . for checking your messages. Tillman never did get to New Mexico.

Shreveport Municipal Auditorium, home of the Louisiana Hayride

The Gladewater Connection

November 22, 1954 - Gladewater - Mint Club

Good morning, Texas. This is radio station K-S-I-J, serving the Gladewater community with "some mo' of yo' favo' right, requested, recorded, cowboy, western, hillbilly folk, and mountain william tunes, with some old un's, new un's, good un's, bad un's, glad un's, and sad uns', leg-a-shaking, toe tapping, knee knocking, tearjerkers. So if you've written in, stick around and listen in, as we get ready to get gone, like a turkey thru the cawn."

DJ Tom Perryman ruled the radio world from his small town in East Texas. Like an IP address in the musical net, Tom knew everyone who knew anyone, especially DJs. And DJs in the fifties arbitrarily determined if a record ever got played. In short, they could make ya', take ya', shake ya', or break ya'.

One morning Tom received a call from his old pal Tillman Franks. Got someone I think you might like, Tillman told the DJ. Not many records, but what there is, is gold. You should have heard the girls screaming their heads off at the Hayride. Intrigued, Perryman told Tillman he knew a dive on Tyler highway where they could slide Elvis in. There's no stage fence, but the bands hardly ever get hit with beer bottles anymore . . . even if they stink.

Done.

And on that note (E sharp), Texas welcomed Elvis to the Lone Star State. (Actually Elvis snuck in the back door in Houston. He popped his head in for a concert in which no one remembered his music or his fuzzy face.)

When Elvis stepped off the Greyhound, he looked like ten miles of bad asphalt. Starved, exhausted, and wrinkled beyond recognition, Elvis even smelled like a man who had been sleeping in a car for a while . . . a very small car. Which in truth, he was. In Shreveport, the agent who supposedly booked his little band for the next two weeks suddenly became blacklisted by the clubs. Elvis and the Blue Moon Boys found themselves stranded in

Remember when...

everyone went around singing "He's a tramp, but I love him," in honor of the release of Disney's *Lady and the Tramp*. Other box office smashes of 1955 included *Mister Roberts*, with Henry Fonda, James Cagney, and Jack Lemmon, and *Oklahoma!*

Louisiana with very little money, no place to stay, and few prospects of a prospect. Some of the Hayride gang dug up a few little gigs around town to earn the boys some gas money and the occasional hamburger. Then Tillman Franks found the job in Gladewater for them. They had just enough money left to throw Elvis on the bus and pay for gas to get Scotty and Bill to East Texas with all the equipment.

Gladewater DJ Tom Perryman and his friend Hal Long met the bedraggled singer at the bus station. He wasn't hard to spot; shockingly dressed anorexics wouldn't come into fashion for several decades. The East Texas gents took Elvis down to the Green Hut café to stuff his face with a burger or two, hoping they didn't have to feed him intravenously. While the young man chowed, Hal made him peel off the prunified jacket. Hal's wife worked at the dry cleaners around the corner. He ran it down there for her to work some magic. Tom checked Elvis into the Res-Mor Motel, so the boy could get some shut-eye before that night's show and preferably a long hot bath as well (with lots of soap).

A couple of hours later with a little rest, a shave, and a freshly pressed jacket (how's that for service?), Elvis reemerged a new man. He sauntered through the once prosperous oil town and found his way to that evening's swanky venue, the Mint Club (not that he could miss it, covered from top to bottom in sickly, three-cents-a-gallon chartreuse ... hence the name).

Tom and Hal's wives stood at the door selling tickets. Elvis introduced himself and ventured into the claustrophobo-joint, spotting Scotty and Bill already assembled on stage. The Mint Club might not be much to look at, but hey, at least it had a stage. A couple of weeks ago, they played a blood drive. There's nothing quite like singing to an audience that passes out after the first song (and they tip you with orange juice and Twinkies).

A clean but well-worn looking crowd propped the bar up, swilling longnecks and jawing loudly. When Tom and Hal arrived well into the set, the situation hadn't changed one iota. Elvis and the boys jammed at record volumes, attempting to drown the conversations around them.

Sir, would you mind putting that beer down for a minute and listening? Gladewater 1954

Yes sir, I was referring to you. Gladewater 1954

Fixin' to visit Bobby Rae after this. Did you hear about what happened yesterday?

Just heard about it from my cousin's uncle. He's the one who sold him the tractor.

Well, Erma Jean said she didn't want to have any more young'ns, anyway. . . .

Tom Perryman leaned against the bar, straining to listen to the music and liking what he heard. He noticed a group of women crowding the stage, giving the lead singer the once over. Their enraptured expressions convinced Tom that he needed to tell a couple of his fellow DJs about this guy. Maybe the kid had a future.

At the break, the girls swarmed Elvis. He gave them autographed pictures for fifty cents and hugs for free. One bold young lady asked if he would mind her taking a picture with him; she just happened to bring her camera. Elvis readily agreed but asked if he could get extra copies to send home to his mama. No problem.

Either out of sympathy or very good business sense, Tom Perryman gave the musicians the entire evening's take, instead of shaving his standard twenty-five percent. The boys wrapped up the concert and returned to the Res-Mor ninety dollars richer.

The next morning while Scotty and Bill snoozed, Elvis strolled around town. He popped into the Roundup, a beer joint, to see what passed for entertainment in other sections of

After the show and at halftime, girls could get "Love Ya', Elvis Presley" scrawled across his glossy 8x10 chest for fifty cents. Boys just got a "Yours." Gladewater 1954

Look at that grin. Oh boy! A girl actually wants to take a picture with me. Gladewater 1954

Gladewater, and later scored some barbecue at the Green Frog to sustain him through the long drive.

Elvis and the boys moved on to Houston to fill an already loaded bill. The show proved a success, and in victory, Elvis wired his share of the proceeds home to his folks, complete with a telegram that read:

HI BABIES. HERE'S THE MONEY TO PAY THE BILLS. DON'T TELL NO ONE HOW MUCH I SENT I WILL SEND MORE NEXT WEEK. THERE IS A CARD IN THE MAIL. LOVE, ELVIS

Meanwhile, Tom Perryman phoned a few select contacts and made plans for Elvis to return to Gladewater at a more lively location.

His earliest publicity shot in the "prom date" style, sold out before West Texas. Courtesy of Polly Webb

The "boy next door" look served as his promo pic for Sun Records until the middle of '55.

Would you let your daughter date this bad boy? Post-discovery headshot, late '55 to '56.

The First Elvis Impersonator

December 3, 1954 - Texarkana - Municipal Auditorium

Carl "Cheesie" Nelson was one of those small town, class-clown types whose ultra-accurate impressions either made you laugh hysterically or cry piteously, depending on whether or not he was impersonating you. His uncanny knack for flawlessly imitating the principal's moral lecture, complete with finger pointing and the crescendo on the second syllable of "del-*ín*-quent," might have led him down the long, dark road to crime, but Cheesie preferred to hone his talent on more challenging subjects, musicians.

Late at night, Cheesie secretly listened to DJ Gene Nobles on WLAC Nashville spin Fats Domino, Little Richard, and the Midnighters for black audiences and hundreds of rebellious white teens. At that time, easy listening and my-dog-has-fleas country music monopolized the mass music market. In the South, R&B kept to its tiny corner of the airways. But in the words of an immortal, times they were a changin', and the dawn of the crossover sat poised on the horizon waiting for the perfect ambassador to escort it into mainstream America.

A new record hit the Melody Shop in Texarkana, and the salesman hollered over to Cheesie, who spent so much time at the local record store, he conducted guided tours.

Hey Cheesie, I got a record here I think you're gonna like.

Spinning on a turntable, the tinny tones of "That's Alright, Mama" filled the listening booth. With its thumping bass and fast licks, the record sounded raw and wild and wholly unlike anything Cheesie had ever heard before. He stopped the record and examined the sunburst on the 45's label. Elvis Presley, who in the world was that?

Setting the record player to automatically repeat, Cheesie practiced the song in the mirror in his room until his rendition reached perfection, surpassing even his impression of Little Richard. Then he took his show on the road, not to Vegas, but to the Texarkana High School talent show. With his friend future recording artist Pat Cupp playing Scotty Moore's part on guitar, Cheesie wowed the crowd with "That's Alright, Mama." As only a minute fraction of the students had ever heard Elvis, Cheesie's true impersonation skill remained unappreciated until three weeks later, when the factory original himself came to Texarkana, backed by his Blue Moon Boys.

Jim LeFann of radio station KOSY sponsored a group of performers to raise the rafters at the Texarkana Memorial Auditorium on December 3. With them, LeFann scribbled in the Hayride rookie Elvis Presley as filler.

The night of the concert, Cheesie sat in the balcony of the auditorium, guarding it, as he often did for Mr. LeFann, from the inevitable deadbeats that tried to sneak in. While Cheesie watched the excited teenagers fill the seats below, another student popped his head in the doorway to inform him that LeFann wanted to speak to him posthaste. Cheesie quickly deputized the recruit and hustled down to the floor.

It seemed that Elvis, Scotty, and Bill were

Texarkana Municipal Auditorium sat geographically on the Arkansas side, but catered almost exclusively to Texans.

Is it live or Memorex? Cheesie does Elvis with Jimmy Day (left), Scotty, D. J. Fontana, and Bill (right). Texarkana 1955. Courtesy of Marileon Hopkins Jerden

running a tad late, Mr. LeFann explained. They needed to stall for time.

Cheesie said nothing, just scratched his crew cut and scuffed his oxfords.

Rumor has it that you do an impression of Elvis, Mr. LeFann continued. How about doing it on stage to warm up the crowd?

Cheesie hesitated. Impersonating someone without their knowledge was one thing; doing it with a better-than-excellent chance that the impersonee might show up in the middle of the act was still another. While Cheesie tried to make up his mind, the local football team hoisted his bean-pole frame in the air and planted it on the stage.

Thus convinced, Cheesie resurrected his talent night entry with pal Pat Cupp, adding a long-suffering version of "Blue Moon of Kentucky" to boot. His act met with great acclaim by the locals, as well as by the new arrival with the sideburns, who laughed his glutious maximus off when he heard the song.

Do you know "Roll With Me Henry?" Elvis asked eagerly as Scotty and Bill hauled their instruments onto stage behind them.

Before Cheesie could finish a nod, Elvis yanked him to the microphone to do a duet, much to the wild approval of their audience. Ladies and gentlemen, Texarkana Municipal Auditorium presents Elvis... in stereo. Blushing, Cheesie slipped into the crowd afterwards, and Elvis continued in monophonic sound for the rest of the evening.

After the concert when Elvis met with the young man again to thank him for his help, Cheesie asked Elvis if he needed him to find a date for the singer. Nineteen-year-old Elvis replied tersely that he could manage on his own. And manage he did, with a chirpy brunette he met after the performance. Like all the kids in town, the two gentlemen cruised to Lee's Drive-In, where Cheesie and Elvis entertained their double dates. Too old for teenie-bop haunts, Scotty and Bill retired to the Townhouse Motel to get some sleep for tomorrow's drive back to Shreveport, where they had a standing

The real enchilada. Texarkana 1955. Courtesy of Marileon Hopkins Jerden

commitment at the Louisiana Hayride.

Cheesie became one of Elvis's "regulars," one of the young people who'd hitch a lift with him whenever the singer played nearby. They double-dated frequently, and their stage duet became a standing order with the audience. By the end of the year, Elvis got in the habit of swinging by the filling station owned by Cheesie's father and asking the young man if he wanted to catch the nearby DeKalb or New Boston show. Is the Pope Catholic? Of course he wanted to go. But fan or no fan, Cheesie's parents wouldn't let him travel to Shreveport to see the Hayride, no matter how sweetly the Memphis boy asked. Maybe they'd heard about Elvis's collection of speeding tickets.

Watch Him Like a Hawk

December 17, 1954 - Hawkins - High School Gymnasium

Hawkins High School, December 1954. Courtesy of Polly Webb

The graduating class of Hawkins High School faced a senior moment; the Class of '54 trip to Panama City, Florida, loomed near, and the fudge sales hadn't raised enough cash to get them even to Longview. So three enterprising young men zipped over to Shreveport on the weekend to catch the Louisiana Hayride and hopefully convince one of its singers to do a show at their alma mater.

One of the new singers of the Hayride broadcast, some guy with the unlikely name of "Elvis," seemed perfect for the job; he was hip, he was now, he was within their limited budget. The three pounced on their victim as he exited the auditorium. Doil Stone, high school senior and future salesman-of-the-year, explained their impoverished situation. Performer and performees struck a deal and sealed it with a handshake. Elvis would play at the Hawkins High School gym in December.

Hawkins High School gym 1954. Courtesy of Polly Webb

And for entertainment, we had olc whatshisname. Hawkins Yearbook 1954. Courtesy of Billy Bob Pruitt

Let's see how many people we can get on one tiny platform. Carolyn Bradshaw, E., and Bill (far right), careful not to step too lively. Hawkins Yearbook 1954. Courtesy of Polly Webb

From Shreveport back to Hawkins, Doil and company had two and a half hours to contemplate how to sell their scheme to the school superintendent, a Baptist deacon.

On a Friday afternoon, Elvis and the Blue Moon Boys wheezed into town in a yellow Bellaire, borrowed from Scotty's wife, Bill's bass strapped to the roof. They rambled up the main drag and turned into the high school parking lot stashed behind the downtown strip. They unloaded the Chevy in the parking lot and, piece by piece, lugged the equipment to the basketball gym, where a narrow two-foot-high platform had spontaneously appeared overnight with the help of some industrious high school elves. While they assembled and tested the mikes, amps, lights, and other band paraphernalia, the town's pride and joy, the Hawkin's Hawks, hooped it up fifteen feet from the stage, preparing to defeat their East Texas rivals with Jordan-esque (or in this case, Cousy-esque) moves. Forty minutes into the practice, the basketball players heard a disembodied voice behind them.

Mind if I play? asked the newcomer with sideburns.

Team captain Billy Bob

Pruitt looked the skinny singer over, sizing up the competition. Sure, he said. Someone, get that kid a jersey and shorts. (Apparently Elvis didn't resemble much of a threat.)

Elvis eventually lured Scotty and Bill into the game, and in the end, the evenings' entertainment retired with a net worth of 20+ points, depending on who's telling the story. Fortunately, NBA scouts were not lurking that day, or history might have turned out very differently.

That night the inhabitants of the Humble Oil town had turned out in groves of droves, some out of curiosity, some because there wasn't much else happening on a Friday night in East Texas. Although that marvelous invention called "television" started making its debut across the country, few homefolk actually owned one. And even if your family splurged and bought a set, the TV signal in most of Texas was still too weak to receive clear images. The good news was that in most of East Texas, you had a choice of three channels, a virtual smorgasbord of selection. The bad news was that they all broadcasted snow.

So most of the population of the oil town turned out, as well as the bored and restless from neighboring villages. At a buck a pop, the school trip to Florida suddenly seemed much closer geographically.

A deliriously happy and financially prosperous Doil Stone and his equally ecstatic co-conspirators welcomed the musicians as the entertainers rolled to a stop in front of the gymnasium. To open the show, Elvis invited petite stunner and on-again off-again girlfriend Carolyn Bradshaw of the Hayride. She was promptly whisked away to the girls' locker room to prepare, as the gentlemen retired to their respective abode to await their cue.

Carolyn Bradshaw, 1954

After a tantalizing period of time, Elvis vaulted to the stage in the memorable pink and black suit that would soon serve as his trademark costume. Leg twitching, he launched into "Hearts of Stone," only to be met with an enthusiastic roar from the pumped-up crowd. Like a foreshadowing of this time next year, girls screamed, cried, and did their impression of pogo sticks in saddle oxfords. Younger girls in the audience laughed at the hysterics of the older girls, and in the back of the auditorium, student Don Dierlam frantically adjusted his new gadget, a reel-to-reel tape recorder, in an early attempt to become a Napster executive. Much to his chagrin, the tape later revealed static, a couple of F sharps, and enough screaming to rival the Roman lion dens.

The jam session ended with a "Shake, Rattle, and Roll," literally. Students, reluctant to lose the concert high, bought souvenir pictures hawked by Bill Black for fifty cents and waited to get the signature of the wild man they had just heard on stage.

Scotty, Elvis, and Bill, freshly scrubbed and still wearing their Starlite Wrangler costumes. Symbolically enough, in later versions of this picture, Elvis no longer has his hands on the friends' shoulders, and after Parker enters the scene, there's no Scotty or Bill either. Courtesy of Johnny Stokes

"How did you like the show?" Elvis asked James Dean wanna-be Lee Taliaferro. Forgetting that he was supposed to act cool, Lee blankly thrust out a couple sheets of mimeograph tests he'd bummed off a friend. Smiling crookedly, Elvis scribbled on them. Lee was elbowed to the back of the crowd before he looked down at the handwriting.

Yours truly, Lash Larue
alias Elvis Presley

Apparently, Lee wasn't the only teenager who wanted to be a movie star.

The lights dimmed, the teenagers migrated homeward, and the musicians packed the car for the long drive to Shreveport. The Louisiana Hayride required them to perform every Saturday, with a strict five-misses-and-you're-out policy. So all were long gone by Sunday, when Deacon Smith rained brimstone on the impious youth of the town for listening to "devil's music." Smith vowed that sinner Presley would never again tarnish their fair high school with his "sexual inn-u-endos." And Elvis never did. He performed at the rec center instead.

Courtesy of Rob Lowe Jr.

Two for the show . . .

New Year's Revelation

Well, if you've seen my milk cow,
Please ride her on home.
I ain't had no milk or butter
Since that cow's been gone.

— from "The Milk Cow Blues Boogie" by K. Arnold, recorded December 20, 1954, by E. Presley

As the new year sailed in, so did Elvis's ship, so to speak. His recent release, "The Milk Cow Blues Boogie" backed with "You're a Heartbreaker," flew off the shelves faster than the clerks could stock them. Pressed in both 45s and 78s, Sun Records wanted to cover both bases, even though 78s had already begun their slipslide into obscurity.

After a couple of months, the Louisiana Hayride seemed like home and all the players like family. The show was broadcast on radio stations throughout East Texas, and the steady Saturday work gave Elvis invaluable exposure as well as $18 per appearance and a chance to refine his stage presence. But it also made the threesome crisscross the states at a frantic pace to meet their commitments.

The November and December stints at the Houston Cook's Hoedown Club opened the door for a series of Houston appearances with paltry but predictable income. True, no one seemed to notice them there before, during, or after the performance. But the paychecks didn't bounce. Scotty and Bill finally quit their day jobs and devoted themselves to their music careers, creating rockabilly widows out of their wives. Elvis quit his job and sent most of his earnings home to his parents.

On New Year's Night, the boys played Houston's Grand Prize Saturday Night Jamboree at Eagles Hall. Elvis sang Ray Charles's "I've Got a Woman" and "Baby, Let's Play House" to a hoard of girls who screamed through the entire set, especially through the lyrics "She knows a woman's place is right there in the home." Go figure.

That same day, Elvis's parents signed the contract with Bob Neal, since their son still legally counted as a minor. Back in October, WMPS DJ Bob Neal had started a dialog with Sam Phillips at Sun Records about possibly managing the boys. Bob had booked Elvis at several locales by this time through Sam, and in November he offered his management expertise to the Hillbilly Cat. After a two-month wait-and-see period, the one-year contract rang in the new year. Bob Neal immediately set to the task of earning his keep and keeping his earn.

Wow! Just love that Alvis Presley!

The next week the Hayride played a whirlwind tour through West Texas, including the senior high school field house in Odessa, the Municipal City Auditorium in San Angelo, and Midland's high school auditorium, before zipping over to East Texas for a January 9 concert at New Boston High School. The turnout remained small but enthusiastic. The music industry might not know what to do with Elvis yet, but the teenagers did.

> *Mama she done told me,*
> *Papa done told me too,*
> *Son, that gal you're foolin' with,*
> *She ain't no good for you.*
>
> — E. Presley, "That's Alright, Mama"

Those Same Old Harbor Lights

January 9, 1955 - New Boston

A colonel at the Red River Army Arsenal swooped home one evening and announced to his wife and to baby-sitter Jo Hawkes they were calling a substitute tot-watcher and were all going out for the evening. The NCO club outside Texarkana had booked a group that held some appeal to teenagers, he heard. The colonel thought that Jo might want an evening off from the infant cadets.

The club already hopped with off-duty personnel when they arrived. The colonel and the two ladies grabbed a table in the corner just before some wild guy with a twitchy leg and a pink suit cranked the heat with his rendition of "Tweedle-Dee." Fourteen-year-old Jo immediately took to the wonderful but radical new sound she heard, and when the Bambi-eyed singer asked her to dance, she agreed, even though she thought he wore the most bizarre color combination she'd ever seen on one human being at one time and detected unmistakable signs of dandruff in the slicked-back hair.

As the musicians gathered their belongings to leave that night, Elvis slid up to the table and asked the colonel if it would be acceptable if he called Jo when he journeyed back to town. The colonel hooked his thumb at the girl and told the suitor, ask her, she's just our baby-sitter.

Jo scribbled her phone number on a napkin for Elvis and left with her employers, the club and its occupants retreating from her young mind as soon as she stepped out the door.

New Boston High School Gymnasium

When Mrs. Hawkes called her daughter to the phone in early January, the last person Jo expected to hear from was the singer from the NCO club. True, she had given him her number, but she didn't really expect him to actually call her. The soft, southern drawl on the line told her that he was booked for a show in New Boston. Did she want to meet him and have a bite afterwards? Jo hesitated. Back in Texarkana, when she impulsively handed over her phone number, Jo had neglected to mention the minor detail of her boyfriend, an insanely jealous football player. Somehow Jo never got around to telling her boyfriend that she had given the handsome singer with the long eyelashes her phone number. But hey, how often in life does one get the chance to schmooze with a rock singer in loud clothes? Jo consented and found herself on the 9th of January on the front row of the New Boston high school gymnasium, watching Elvis croon "Harbor Lights" significantly in her direction.

After the show, Elvis and Jo migrated to Keathley's Drive-in, the local teenage shake & date spot. At a spare table inside, they munched on a wholesome meal of 10W-30 weight burgers, french fries with vinegar, cherry Cokes, and Brown Cows (for the added nutrition). The jukebox beckoned to Elvis, who stared into its depths for a few moments before popping a

I longed to hold you dear,
And kiss you just once more.
But you were on the ship,
And I was on the shore.

—from "Harbor Lights" by Williams and Kennedy

Anne Braley (left), Jo Hawkes, E., and the picture with a short lifespan. DeKalb 1955. Courtesy of Willie Cox

handful of nickels into the glowing face. "That's Alright, Mama" by E. Presley blasted out of the wooferless speakers . . . seven times in succession. Just as Jo contemplated whether her date was euphoric that one of his records graced a jukebox along with Hank Williams and Ernest Tubb, or the most conceited jerk she'd ever met, her cousin Pat stared at them through the frosty window. Painfully shy, Pat stood in the parking lot and waited for her chance to talk to the singer that she had become infatuated with in Texarkana last month. The occasion never presented itself.

Elvis drove Jo home, and they smooched goodbye until the porchlight flashed on imperatively. He asked her if he could call her again when he played the area. Still floating on a post-kiss high, Jo melted in agreement. As he drove off, she walked in the front door, only to find her mother and boyfriend waiting for her with crossed arms and tapping feet.

In March when Jo's mother reluctantly handed the phone to her, Elvis announced his

DeKalb Gymnasium

E. and the boys play on a truck flatbed, the latest thing in mobile stages. New Boston, April 1955. Courtesy of Willie Cox

DeKalb performance. This time as reinforcement against her weakening will, she dragged friend Anne Braley to play chaperone. After the show, Elvis volunteered to sign a photo for the girls, which Jo had never thought to ask for before. That photograph lived a very short life. In the days after the DeKalb assignation, Jo and her boyfriend launched into a pitched battle over strange singers, who shall be nameless but whose initials are E.P., arriving in town and dating certain local females at certain infamous burger joints for all the world to see. The boyfriend ripped the photo into microscopic fragments.

Jo never saw Elvis again after that night. When he called for the New Boston show in April, Jo's mother tersely informed the suitor that Jo could no longer see him; she would be washing her hair . . . indefinitely. Mrs. Hawkes neglected to mention that Jo had just recently become Mrs. Photoripper.

"I'm leaving town for sure. Well, then you won't be bothered with me hangin' 'round your door." New Boston, April 1955. Courtesy of Willie Cox

In January 1955 -
USS *Nautilus*, the first nuclear powered sub, took its first test dive in the Long Island Sound.

That's Ol' right, Mama

January 24, 1955 - Hawkins - Humble Oil Camp

Meanwhile, in that thriving urban metropolis of Hawkins, rock-a-billy convert Doil Stone heard that East Texas would host Elvis for a winter tour starting the end of January. Tom Perryman, DJ and canny station manager at KSIJ Radio in Gladewater, had already scheduled the young singer in Tyler and Gilmer, and Doil contrived to drag Elvis back to Hawkins, even though his own soul would surely catch the express train to the fiery pit of eternal damnation, according to Deacon Smith. Doil, however, was Hawkin's star pitcher, and it just so happens that his team manager, Don Franks, was a bigwig in Humble Oil and Refinery, the company that placed their fair town on the map and put the ol' in ol' ya'll.

Like many towns in Texas, Hawkins owed its existence to the miraculous sludge found deep under the red clay; oil that is, Black Gold, Texas Tea. After its explosive discovery at the turn of the century, companies tripped over themselves to stake their claims from the Panhandle to the Gulf of Mexico. But the Big Three: the Texas Company now known as Texaco; the one named for the nearby body of water, Gulf Oil Corporation; and Humble Oil, (a.k.a. Esso, a.k.a. Exxon, a.k.a. ExxonMobil) reined supreme. Together, they carved the state into viability sectors . . . too deep, potential, moderate find, and thar' she blows! Oil camps, towns inhabited solely by the oil company employees and their families, popped up in every corner of Texas. The colonists enjoyed all the perks their bountiful employers bestowed upon them; cheap groceries, inexpensive or free housing, a rotation of regular entertainment, and best of all, free gasoline for life.

So when Doil Stone asked Don Franks for his permission to allow Elvis to play their town, the Humble Oil executive granted his blessing, his influence, and the recreation hall in the oil camp.

On January 24 Elvis and his two sidekicks traveled the winding roads through the Piney Woods of East Texas to begin the winter tour in front of his earliest groupies. Just like before, Elvis received a generous 80 percent of the proceeds. All devotees paid a modest dollar. That's three new freshly minted 45s; eight gallons of gas if you have to pay for it, 1¼ hours of baby-sitting; eight movies, four cartoons, and four newsreels; or two autographed pictures of the King before he became royalty.

Concerned that Elvis might not pull a large enough crowd by himself, Tom Perryman booked popular country singers Jim Ed and Maxine Brown to pad the ticket. He needn't have worried. The little rec hall only held 150, and those teenagers were stuffed in that night like color-coordinated sardines. Kids hung in the open windows and reclined on the grounds around the building as the hillbilly jam thumped the wooden walls and echoed off the

Recreation Hall, Hawkins Oil Camp 1955. Courtesy of Polly Webb

adjoining live oaks, giving Tyler a taste of the treat awaiting them the following evening. The performers played their entire repertoire, but the enthusiastic crowd begged them to stay just five more minutes, and then five minutes more.

Long after the bass lay packed in its case and the others escaped to the Res-Mor Motel in Gladewater, Elvis leaned against the ancient piano and sang the gospel hymns he cut his teeth on. The Hawkins kids urged him to sing slowly so they could appreciate his beautiful voice, and to save the strain on his throat, which hinted at a full-blown bout of laryngitis.

Elvis autographed pictures for the high school students, pictures for visitors from surrounding cities who planned to catch the show two nights later in Gilmer, pictures for girlfriends who were too shy to ask for his autograph, and at the urging of some of the basketball players, a picture for pretty Lavada Robinson, which bore the inscription:

Yours
'til your drawers drop
- Elvis Presley

She was not amused. Stomping off, Lavada threatened to tell Don Franks of the insult on her person.

Elvis never played Hawkins again; no one truly knows why not. No matter, nearly every Hawkins inhabitant under twenty years of age appeared at any of his performances within a fifty-mile radius. They piled into their Chevys and sat on each other's laps for two-plus-hour drives to Louisiana or Texarkana. So many of them appeared at his concert in Gilmer, he inquired politely of the crowd, "Am I in Hawkins?"

Before he went back to the motel in Gladewater that night, he signed stacks of photos until his pen ran out of ink.

Elvis borrowed Don Frank's classy corporate pen, given to him for meritorious service above and beyond the call of duty. Not until Elvis was pj'd and tucked in at the Res-Mor did Franks realize his pen had been accidentally kidnapped by the singer in an open and shut case of klepto-scribo. Fourteen miles later, Franks retrieved his prize possession, none the worse for wear and with no ransom paid.

Greatly influenced by his idol, in years to come Doil Stone formed a band of his own, changing his name to Buddy Miller because his father feared someone would discover he had accidentally spawned a musician. Buddy Miller and the Rocking Ramblers rearranged the old Hank Ballard number "The Twist," recorded it, and sent a copy to Dick Clark in hopes that he would play it on that new television program *American Bandstand.* Instead, Clark gave it to a virtual unknown in the business named Chubby Checker, who subsequently did play it on *Bandstand,* under his own name.

Elvis moved on to Tyler and later to stardom, and eventually the faithful piano moved across town to the church, where it sat next to the pulpit. For years to come, whenever Deacon Smith preached from his perch on the inherent dangers of rock and roll, he unwittingly placed his hand on the very same spot "sinner Presley" laid his when he sang those lovely hymns that night in Hawkins. How's that for poetic justice?

A' dairing Encounter

January 25, 1955 - Tyler - Mayfair Building, Fairgrounds

The next morning Elvis hopped in the car to visit his friend and sponsor, Tom Perryman at KSIJ radio. The station and the Perryman household became home base for the East Texas tour. Billie, Tom's wife, fed Elvis nan'er pudding and washed his one stage shirt after each performance. Sometimes he stayed at their house when the Res-Mor became overbooked during the "tourist" season.

Elvis practiced in the beautiful tropical wood-lined sound studio at the radio station, and later Tom interviewed him to gab about last night's shindig in Hawkins and to promote the upcoming show in Tyler that evening. Unfortunately, due to the standard procedure of overwriting "worthless" recordings, very few of these pitches remain for posterity.

By 8 p.m. the Mayfair building on the Tyler fairground burst with excitement. Many of Hawkins' rebellious youth piled into cars to see the show again that night, and numbers of Tyler representatives, who danced on the rec hall's lawn, returned to bop in their own fair city. The sum of

Radio KSIJ serving the Gladewater community.

the crowd consisted of the curious, the bored, and the defiant looking for a hot time on a school night.

One such lurker, Lois Adair, only attended because her friend Betty Bailey dragged her. Good girls didn't frequent concerts by themselves.

Jim Ed and Maxine wound up their segment, and Elvis bounded onto the stage. Lois stood transfixed.

Oh God, he's beautiful!

Oblivious to the sound emanating from the little boy face, Lois applauded with the rest to keep him on stage so she could look at him a while longer. Before the last chord was struck, Lois became determined to get that man's picture. She grabbed Betty's arm and dragged her through the crowd. Backstage, they elbowed themselves up to the table where Bill Black sold photographs for $1, and Elvis signed them. Lois dredged the bottom of her purse: one tube of lipstick, one clean hanky, a bottle of nail polish borrowed from a friend, two dimes, two quarters, and a nickel. Seventy-five cents; she was short a quarter. Lois dug deeper. She found some lint and an abused aspirin, but no more money. Next to her, Betty's look of despair told Lois that she couldn't cough up any spare finances for her pal. Lois resumed her search and dive expedition but only rescued a safety pin. Over the top of her purse, her eyes met those of Elvis, who had been watching her with a lopsided smile. He proffered her a quarter, which she graciously accepted. Betty took their picture, and when they backed out of the crowd, Lois thought she'd probably never see him again.

The following August, Elvis played the Mayfair building again. After the show, a small crowd collected around the piano where he played with apparently no urgency to leave. When his velvet tenor slid into "Amazing Grace." Lois melted onto the piano bench with him. She decided then and there that he wasn't just a pretty face after all.

Later that night, as teenagers cruised up Broadway, made a U-turn at Webber's, and chugged back down Broadway, Derrick Drive-In and Fuller's Drive-In bustled with business. With 8,000 inhabitants, Tyler boasted *two* full-time drive-ins, but only

Fuller's had an indoor restaurant as well. Carhops zigzagged between finned Chevys, and kids galloped across the gravel to meet their friends just pulling in for a shake. Over the darting hoards, Elvis spotted Lois gossiping with her inner circle.

After the initial introductions, Lois's friends gabbed excitedly with the singer but eventually drifted away to tell other friends who they had just bumped into. Left alone for the moment, Elvis asked Lois if he could give her a lift back to her house and visit for a spell. After a slight hesitation, Lois ducked inside to call her mother. She asked if she could bring home this singer she'd met. He was very nice, very handsome, and she thought he seemed a little homesick.

Absolutely NOT!

From KWKH's
Louisiana Hayride
Tom Perryman of KSIJ
Presents
ELVIS
PRESLEY
SUN RECORDS: "That's Alright Mama" — "Blue Moon of Kentucky"
With
SCOTTY & BILL
Along With
J. E. and MAXINE
BROWN

ELVIS PRESLEY

TUESDAY NIGHT—JAN. 25th
MAYFAIR BUILDING FAIR GROUNDS
8:00 P.M.

ADULTS 1.00 — CHILDREN 50c

Monday, Jan. 24—Hawkins, Texas—Humble Camp Recreation Hall
$1.00 Per Person—8 P.M.
Wednesday, Jan. 26—Gilmer, Texas—REA Bldg. 7:30 P.M.
Students 50c—Adults 1.00
Thursday, Jan. 27—Longview, Texas—Reo Palm Isle Club
1.00 Per Person
Friday, Jan. 28—Gaston HI School—8 P.M.
Students 50c—Adults 1.00

Jailhouse Rock? Tyler Mayfair Building

Her mother's definitive reply sizzled over the telephone wires, torching the tail feathers of comfortably perched birds. Reluctantly, Lois politely declined his offer.

A year later when that nice young man topped the record charts and appeared on the Dorsey Show, Lois decided to visit him at one of his last performances at the Hayride. Her mission, should she choose to accept it, was to get the photograph signed that Betty took of Lois and Elvis together. Much had changed in one year. Instead of hanging around after the show talking to girls, Elvis hid from the groupies who swarmed him. After his performance, Lois tried to visit backstage, but her path was barred by a security guard with strict rules that under no circumstances will any teenagers, especially of the female persuasion, bother Mr. Presley.

Nature triumphed, however. When the guard sneezed, she flung her 5 foot 2 form past his half-turned back and pelted backstage. Realizing his quarry had fled, he lumbered after her, but she had already reached a congregation of performers. Elvis looked up as she skidded to a stop, the guard panting in hot pursuit. "That's all right, I know this one," the man in pink told the grumbling guard.

Lois never saw Elvis face to face again after that night, but she can content herself with her hard-won autograph, a kiss from a lonely musician, and a great story to tell her customers at the Deep Ellum burger bistro she now owns in Dallas.

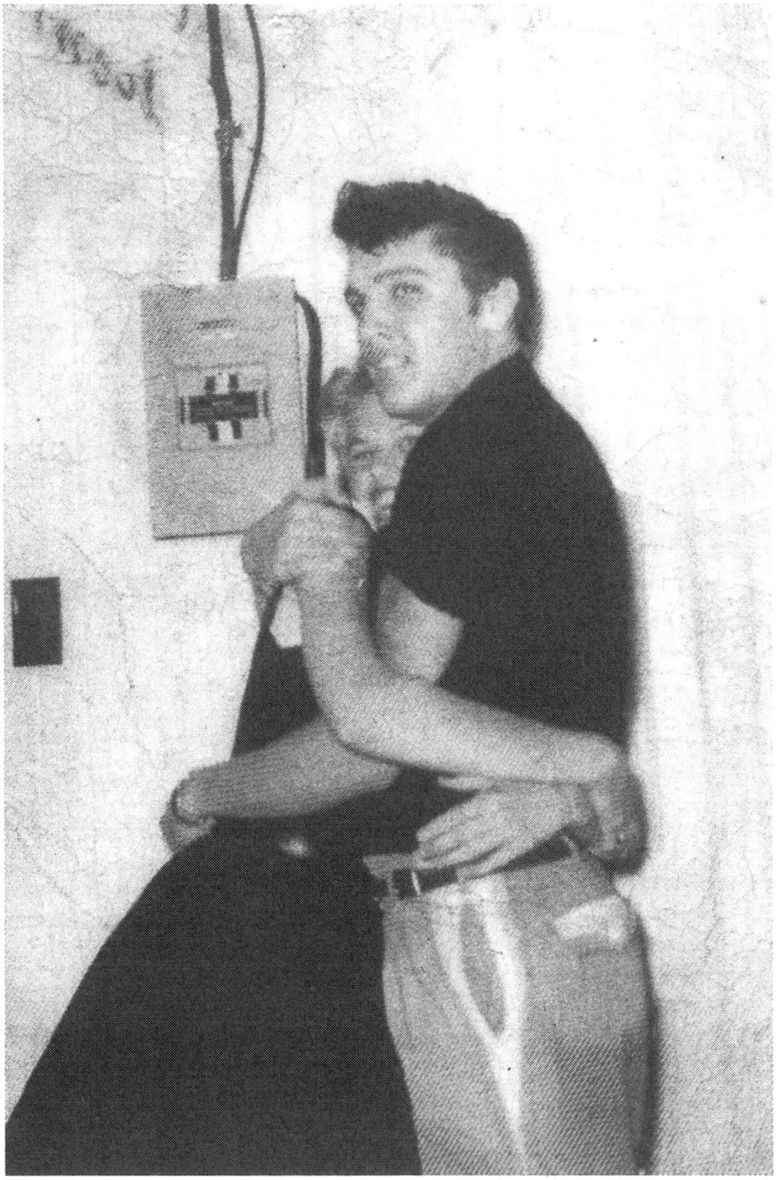

Brother, can you spare a quarter? Lois Adair and E. share a hug. Tyler 1955. Courtesy of Lois Adair

"Am I in Hawkins?"

January 26, 1955 - Gilmer - Rural Electric Co-op Admin. Building

Three days into the East Texas winter tour, Elvis, Scotty, and Bill left Tyler and tooled up Highway 155, past the stock ponds and cattle staring unimpressed at passersby. The white pines on either side of the winding road magically transformed the land into a green oasis in the dead of winter, as if North Carolina suddenly planted itself in the middle of the state. Gilmer, the site of their next performance, lay just a leisurely piece up the road. With no tractors to pass on the two-lane road during winter, they made it to Gilmer with plenty of time to grab a bite at the White Swan Café.

They sauntered into the café, Elvis sporting long sideburns and a pink and red checkered sport jacket. The eyes of Texas followed them to their booth. Either they were some new kind of musicians, or the circus had snuck back into town.

Like his music, Elvis's style drew heavily from the African-American rhythm and blues culture. He bought all his clothes at Lanskey's in Memphis, a store not usually frequented by white southern boys. In a time when the Pat Boone white button-down was the accepted norm, the bright colors and be-bop sound simultaneously shocked and attracted audiences into taking notice. But if the old phrase, "good girls fell for Pat Boone, bad girls fell for Elvis" stood true, then 90 percent of the female population of the fifties were bad girls.

Acquiring a table, the threesome politely ordered their supper from the wary waitress. Every spoonful of chili and pie closely scrutinized, the locals waited breathlessly for the telltale disturbing behavior indicative of rock-a-billy singers, as they suspected these men to be. After two courses and quantities of iced tea, not so much as a gun had been brandished. The disappointed Gilmer inhabitants watched the strangers eat and leave, displaying no outward signs of mental instability . . . until that evening.

The performance hall connected to the Gilmer Rural Electrical Co-op held about 150 but sported a real stage, an impressive addition for a town of just over 4,000. Surrounding the stage sat two rows composed entirely of Hawkins's devotees chattering excitedly until the Browns started the program. Having caught the show on Monday in Hawkins, the teenagers decided to see it again on Wednesday in Gilmer, where they could still buy tickets. The perennial favorites Jim Ed and Maxine Brown primed the audience. About half of the turnout came to hear them but were willing to listen to the newcomer Presley play those strange up-tempo blues songs. Meanwhile, the kids from Hawkins waited patiently for the Browns to leave the stage so their newly crowned favorite musician could take the stage. They weren't disappointed.

Jim Ed and Maxine Brown

When the last chords of the Browns' harmony faded, Elvis and the Blue Moon Boys vaulted to the stage. Taking their places, left, right, and center, Bill spun his bass and slung hokey, Dixie-cup humor to warm up both the crowd and Elvis, who notoriously got the jitters before performing. When the audience heated to a rolling boil, Bill stepped forward and wound Elvis with an invisible key, jumping back just in time to miss the leg that started quivering to the screams of the girls in the audience. The leg twitched wildly and the volume cranked to eardrum-bursting level. When his hips started jerking, the pounding decibels of "That's Alright, Mama" were drowned completely by the atonal shrieks of hormone-effluent females. Fortunately for the performers, an overflow of estrogen apparently makes one tone deaf, because Elvis's strained voice cracked multiple times during his songs. The case of laryngitis that had threatened for days finally took up residence in his throat, a point not overlooked by the neglected boyfriends in the audience.

To save the wear and tear on his voice, Elvis deputized Johnny Stokes, one of the Hawkins zealots who caught every performance within a fifty-mile radius, into selling autographed photos for him for the customary buck a pop. Johnny took to the task with the vigor of a sideshow barker. For his trouble, he received two signed photos and fair commission for the sales. Johnny would have done it for free, but somehow he never got around to telling Elvis that fact.

Gilmer Rural Electric Cooperative Administration Building

Longview or Bust ... or Both

January 27, 1955 - Longview - Reo Palm Isle Club

Detroit showroom or Longview club? Reo Palm Isle Club, Longview, January 1955

On January 27 the group was scheduled to play the Reo Palm Isle, a hugely popular club known for launching stellar careers if you could fill the 1,800 seats that it boasted. Glen Keeling, the owner, booked the boys as a personal favor to DJ Tom Perryman, even though he had never heard of this "Elvis guy." But Reo sales ran sluggish on Thursdays, and the cost of the drinks alone would pay the rent for the evening. The band could split the ticket sales, if there were any.

To hedge his bets, Tom Perryman invited about a hundred friends to the club for the show. They obligingly showed; such was the power of a DJ in the fifties. However, almost no one else did. The troop played to a lukewarm scattering of 160 people. None of the Hawkins kids showed. The Reo Palm Isle was a tad too ritzy for the teenage purse and Longview a tad too far to drive on a school night. Besides, everyone knew that the Reo served alcohol, right out in the open, yet.

After the show Elvis circulated through the tables and chatted with folk as he customarily liked to do. One of the few ladies to ask for a photograph that night asked him how he was doing, to which he replied honestly, "If something doesn't happen pretty soon, I'm going to have to go back to driving a truck."

As the boys prepared to leave that evening, Elvis stole a glance at Keeling's new Ford Crown Victoria painted in limited edition (very limited edition) Tropical Rose.

I sure do like the color of that car, Elvis told the owner.

The next time Keeling saw Elvis, the young man drove a pink Cadillac.

Band-Aide at Joinerville

January 28, 1955 - Joinerville - Gaston High School Auditorium

Get out before we throw you out. The Res-Mor Motel in Gladewater

One more stop on the East Texas tour and the weary compadres could vamoose home. The band checked themselves out of the Res-Mor Motel in Gladewater on the morning of the 28th, neither party too choked up about the parting. Not exactly the Ritz Carlton, Res-Mor was the only motel within a thirty-mile radius, so either the threesome slept there or on the street.

The owners of the Res-Mor, for their part, couldn't wait to get rid of the musicians. Several times they'd threatened to boot them out if the boys didn't clean up their act. The King was one heck of a singer, but two hecks of a slob.

The town of Joinerville sat seven miles west of Henderson during its oil boom in the thirties. Until "Dad" Joiner sold the Daisy Bradford Number 3 to H. L. Hunt of Dallas, Joinerville floated atop the largest oil field in the world. In the 1950s, when their neighbor New London literally blew itself off the map, Gaston High School gathered both towns' children into its hallowed halls.

Wallace Read, the band director of the high school, along with several of the band's parents racked their brains for a fundraiser that would actually make money for a change, no pun intended. One day the parents barged into Read's office with a dazzling idea. Some young guy named Presley had wowed them at Hawkins last month. For 60 percent of the proceeds, Presley could play at their high school auditorium. Apparently the kids liked him for some reason. Read had never heard of this guy. He never listened to that Hayride hillbilly stuff if he could help it. Give him Gershwin any day. Nevertheless, Read agreed to speak to Superintendent Duran, and if no objections were raised, they might be able to slide Presley in for a performance in late January.

Tom Perryman scribbled Elvis down for the night of January 28 in Joinerville. A final night of the East Texas tour in the town would get Presley back to Shreveport to play at the Hayride the following night. Eager for a smaller, more enthusiastic venue than the previous night's Longview fiasco, Elvis, Scotty, and Bill arrived early to scope out the town. Since downtown Joinerville retained about six businesses, the tour was noticeably brief:

"Welcome to Joinerville - Population ~~1,500~~ ~~800~~ ~~600~~ ~~500~~ 300 and still growing"

post office,
high school,
barber shop,
"Y'all come back, now."

The threesome pulled into a dirt lot. Scotty and Bill took a midwinter's snooze in the car, while Elvis killed time by wandering over to the high school. He bumped into the band director, who took it upon himself to show the new arrival around.

After touring the gymnasium, the two finally parked themselves in the band room, Elvis plinking absentmindedly on the piano while they talked. Read happily informed the young singer that the performance had sold out. The enthusiastic students sold over 600 tickets, far more than the auditorium actually could hold. Fire marshals not being what they are today, the two gentlemen had a great deal to smile about. Elvis became psyched; 600 people at a dollar a piece times 60 percent meant a nice healthy paycheck for the end of the East Texas Tour, even if he had to divide it among the troups and pay for his own records, pictures, and equipment. He graciously thanked the band director, who decided he liked the pleasant, respectful young man, even if his music was strange.

That evening as Mr. Read, Superintendent Duran, their wives, and 600 excited teenagers looked on, the quiet,

Gaston High School

well-mannered boy from that afternoon disappeared into a fiend in a pink suit. Rocketing onstage, Elvis started to quiver like an epileptic. The kids' screams encouraging him, Elvis jerked his head and stared at the audience, forelock falling over his face. They screamed louder. He grunted, and the place exploded. Girls jumped up and down as the man on the stage shook from side to side. Hardly any sound cleared the high-pitched squeals.

Embarrassed by the gyrations on stage, Read turned to apologize to his superintendent. But Duran smiled like a Cheshire cat, rocking back and forth on his heels, dollar signs illuminating his eyes... cha-ching.

As the band broke for intermission, students mobbed Elvis, wanting to talk to him, touch him, get an autograph. Mr. Read watched the boy very closely for the second half. Wish I was his manager, he thought for the first but definitely not the last time.

After the show Read told the young man that he thought his talent was quite something, and he felt Elvis would really make it. Little did he know how right he was.

Less than a year later, Elvis had become a star, shining on national television. On a band trip in Houston, Read bumped into Elvis outside the Hotel Rice. Elvis recognized the band director immediately, a fact that stunned Read. They had only met once for a couple of hours. But Elvis always had an uncanny recall of people he'd once met. Elvis asked if Read had come to see the show, and the teacher replied honestly that he didn't even know Elvis was playing there. The two parted company and continued their separate paths, the teacher once again returning to his original assessment, the polite young man did indeed have a future, even if he didn't play Gershwin.

In February 1955 -
A Senate committee declared that comic books were contributing to rising rates of juvenile delinquency and served merely to teach youngsters "short courses in crime."

It's 8 p.m., Do You Know Where Your Singer Is?

February 10, 1955 - Alpine - Alpine High School Auditorium

Alpine High School, now the junior high.

Mr. Hendrick, we have a small problem with tonight's benefit.

Did you book the singers?

Yes, sir.

Order the posters?

Yep.

Hire the local talent?

Check.

Sell the tickets?

What we could.

Then what's the problem?

The show is about to start and the lead act isn't here yet.

The little hand chugged past eight and the big hand bungee jumped off the twelve and dove down the starboard side of the clock. The "local talent" started to warm the crowd up at the top of the hour, but behind the stage at the Future Farmers of America benefit, an Elvis-sized hole stood in place of a real singer. John Nelson, DJ of KVLF, the "voice of the Last Frontier" in Alpine Texas, began to fret. Audiences aren't green beans; you can't put them on simmer for an hour and expect them to continue to swim contentedly among themselves. Also, green beans don't own pitchforks, Future Farmers do.

For the last month John had finagled with Bob Neal by phone, letter, and telegram to get a group that the locals would cough up some much-needed revenue to see. The manager assured Nelson that Elvis would raise the roof and the capital. All was arranged, despite the lack of PA system, the small auditorium, and some last minute alterations.

Always the considerate employee, John shared his headache with his boss, station manager George Hendrick. After a few moments' deliberation on the virtue of timeliness, Hendrick told John, you take the high road and I'll take the low road and I'll be in Alpine before ye'. Maybe the singers thought they were supposed to play at some other Alpine High School in West Texas. The

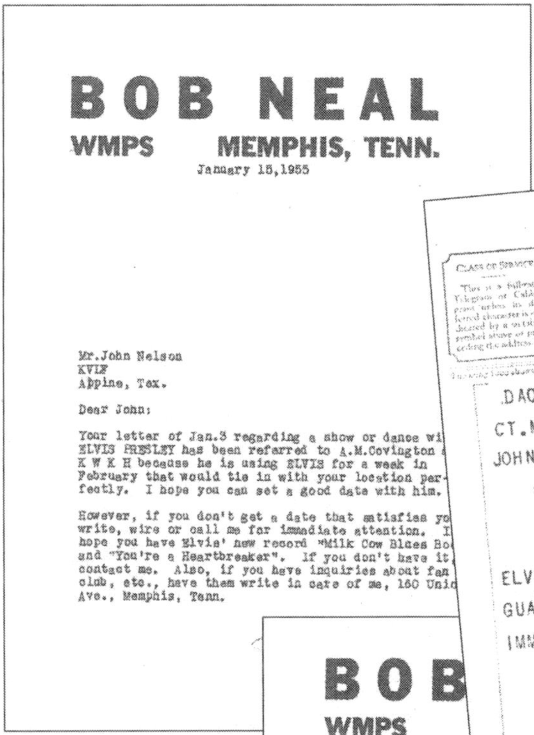

BOB NEAL

WMPS MEMPHIS, TENN.

January 15,1955

Mr.John Nelson
KVLF
Alpine, Tex.

Dear John:

Your letter of Jan.3 regarding a show or dance wi
ELVIS PRESLEY has been referred to A.M.Covington
K W K H because he is using ELVIS for a week in
February that would tie in with your location per-
fectly. I hope you can set a good date with him.

However, if you don't get a date that satisfies yo
write, wire or call me for immediate attention. I
hope you have Elvis' new record "Milk Cow Blues Bo
and "You're a Heartbreaker". If you don't have it,
contact me. Also, if you have inquiries about fan
club, etc., have them write in care of me, 160 Unio
Ave., Memphis, Tenn.

An original "Dear John" letter.
Courtesy of Ms. Traci Nelson Dockery

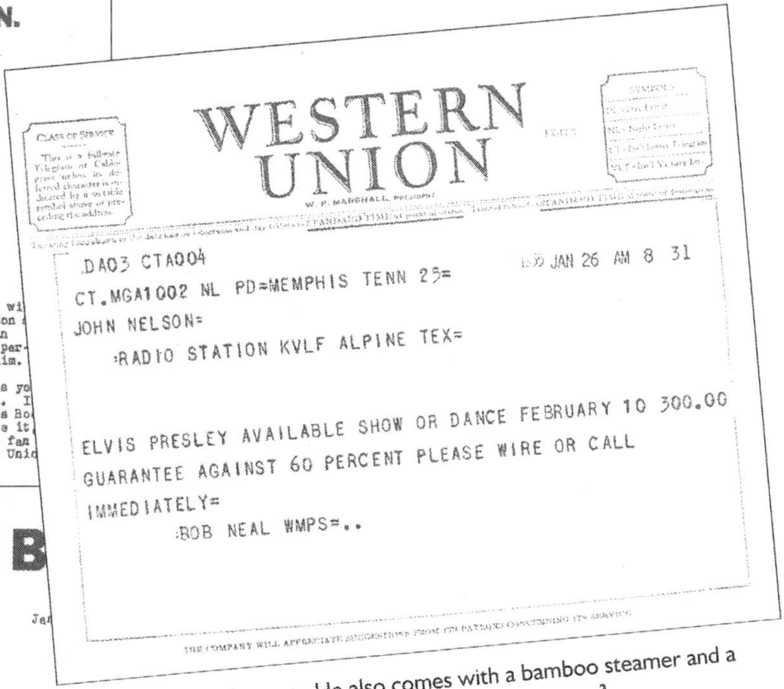

WESTERN UNION

DA03 CTA004 1955 JAN 26 AM 8 31

CT.MGA1002 NL PD=MEMPHIS TENN 25=

JOHN NELSON=

:RADIO STATION KVLF ALPINE TEX=

ELVIS PRESLEY AVAILABLE SHOW OR DANCE FEBRUARY 10 300.00
GUARANTEE AGAINST 60 PERCENT PLEASE WIRE OR CALL
IMMEDIATELY=
:BOB NEAL WMPS=..

But wait, don't order now. He also comes with a bamboo steamer and a handy set of steak knives. Now how much would you pay?
Courtesy of Ms. Traci Nelson Dockery

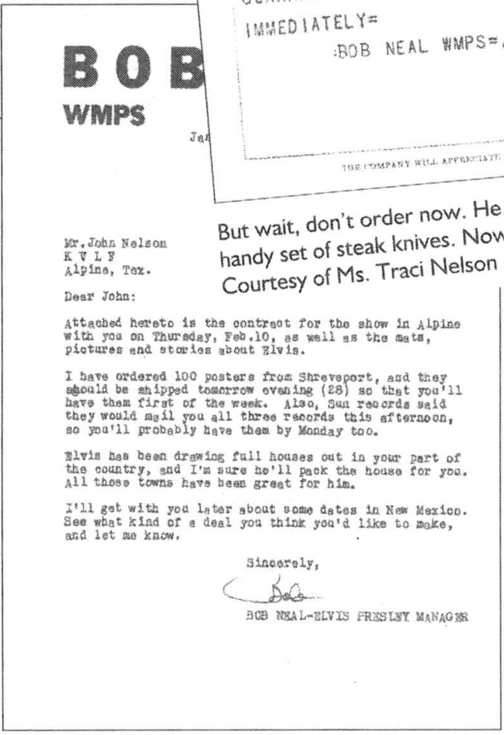

BOB

WMPS

Ja

Mr.John Nelson
K V L F
Alpine, Tex.

Dear John:

Attached hereto is the contract for the show in Alpine
with you on Thursday, Feb.10, as well as the mats,
pictures and stories about Elvis.

I have ordered 100 posters from Shreveport, and they
should be shipped tomorrow evening (28) so that you'll
have them first of the week. Also, Sun records said
they would mail you all three records this afternoon,
so you'll probably have them by Monday too.

Elvis has been drawing full houses out in your part of
the country, and I'm sure he'll pack the house for you.
All those towns have been great for him.

I'll get with you later about some dates in New Mexico.
See what kind of a deal you think you'd like to make,
and let me know.

Sincerely,

BOB NEAL-ELVIS PRESLEY MANAGER

Courtesy of Ms. Traci Nelson Dockery

two grabbed their coats and slipped out the door unnoticed.

In ever-widening circles, Hendrick and Nelson scoured the gravel roads around their fair town. Their heavy cars tore past the rough terrain, strewn with tumbled boulders from the nearby Chalk Mountains. All appeared haunted in the cold winter twilight.

Nelson began to worry that something had happened to the young men. West Texas could be a very remote place if broken down or lost, and the winter night creeping in on them felt as cold as ever-loving Christmas.

On their third pass, Nelson spotted the weary travelers kicking the tires of their car both in frustration and possibly to keep warm. The old Chevy lay in a fetal position on the side of the road, its hood and front fender bruised and aching from the collision they'd inadvertently participated in outside Alpine. After Bill's CPR, Scotty's abuse, and Elvis's sweet talk, their faithful steed wheezed back to life. The threesome managed to kick it at a slow clop into Alpine, where it probably had

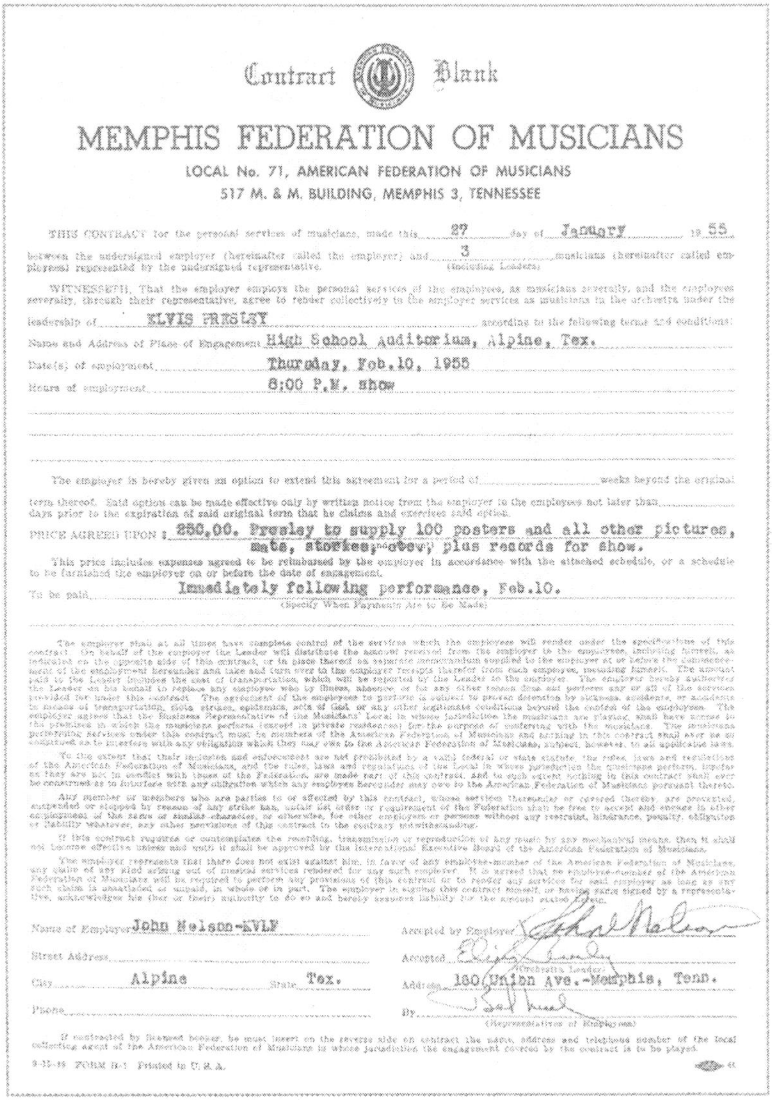
Contract Blank

MEMPHIS FEDERATION OF MUSICIANS

LOCAL No. 71, AMERICAN FEDERATION OF MUSICIANS

517 M. & M. BUILDING, MEMPHIS 3, TENNESSEE

THIS CONTRACT for the personal services of musicians, made this 27 day of January 19 55

between the undersigned employer (hereinafter called the employer) and 3 (Including Leaders) musicians (hereinafter called employees) represented by the undersigned representative.

WITNESSETH, That the employer employs the personal services of the employees, as musicians severally, and the employees severally, through their representative, agree to render collectively to the employer services as musicians in the orchestra under the leadership of ELVIS PRESLEY according to the following terms and conditions:

Name and Address of Place of Engagement High School Auditorium, Alpine, Tex.

Date(s) of employment Thursday, Feb.10, 1955

Hours of employment 8:00 P.M. show

The employer is hereby given an option to extend this agreement for a period of ______ weeks beyond the original term thereof. Said option can be made effective only by written notice from the employer to the employees not later than ______ days prior to the expiration of said original term that he claims and exercises said option.

PRICE AGREED UPON $ 250.00. Presley to supply 100 posters and all other pictures, mats, stories, etc., plus records for show.

This price includes expenses agreed to be reimbursed by the employer in accordance with the attached schedule, or a schedule to be furnished the employer on or before the date of engagement.

To be paid Immediately following performance, Feb.10.
(Specify When Payments Are to Be Made)

[illegible]

Name of Employer John Nelson-KVLF

Street Address

City Alpine State Tex.

Phone

Accepted by Employer [signature]

Accepted [signature] (Orchestra Leader)

Address 180 Union Ave.-Memphis, Tenn.

By [signature] (Representatives of Employees)

If contracted by licensed booker, he must insert on the reverse side on contract the name, address and telephone number of the local collecting agent of the American Federation of Musicians in whose jurisdiction the engagement covered by the contract is to be played.

9-35-55 FORM B-1 Printed in U.S.A.

$250 sounds like a lot of money in the fifties until you read the fine print of this standard musicians' contract. Elvis had to divide the money among his own band and provide his own records and marketing materials when he played Alpine, unless of course he was detained due to "sickness, accidents, riots, strikes, epidemics or Acts of God."

It looks like Bel Keeel (Bob Neal) and Elixir Pusly badly needed to attend handwriting school, except that Elvis didn't actually sign this contract. Bob Neal signed it for him.

Courtesy of Ms. Traci Nelson Dockery

a great deal to complain about to the other cars in the lot.

Despite the circumstances and the sparse ticket sales, Elvis, Scotty, and Bill played an encore performance to a small but feisty audience. As if galvanized by the post-collision adrenaline high, the threesome let it all hang out. John Nelson introduced the group and Scotty and Bill galloped into their positions on stage. After a pause carefully designed to drive the masses wild, Elvis oozed onto stage and gave them a sultry stare from bedroom eyes. Galvanized by the look, the women bubbled screams like estrogen percolators. Elvis executed his trademark "snap and jerk," launching into an upbeat hillbilly repertoire unlike anything these West Texas folks had ever heard. He twisted back and forth to the music, glancing occasionally over his shoulder at John Nelson, who still stood rooted to the stage, transfixed.

Elvis wasn't the only one who noticed the lurker; Hendrick hissed at the DJ from the sidelines. After several attempts, Hendrick diverted Nelson's attention just long enough to send him the psychic message, "get off the stage, John." In case the vibes got jumbled on the way through the cosmosphere, Hendrick jerked an impatient thumb toward the side of the stage. John shook himself back to reality and scuttled off the stage. The band rocked on.

After the performance, Elvis signed records and photos for the excited teens. With very little coaxing, he succumbed to autographing the petticoat of the banker's daughter. After an hour or so, Scotty, Bill, and the Nelsons

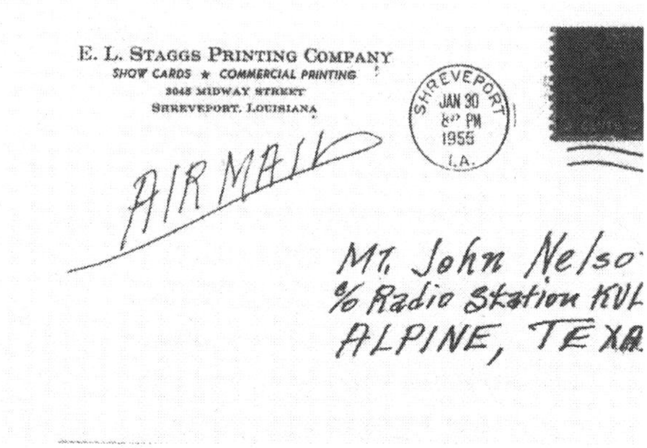

Ah, the days when you could mail a letter with no address and no zip code, and still the letter would get there the next day. Postmarked 8 p.m. no less; someone was working late that night. Courtesy of Ms. Traci Nelson Dockery

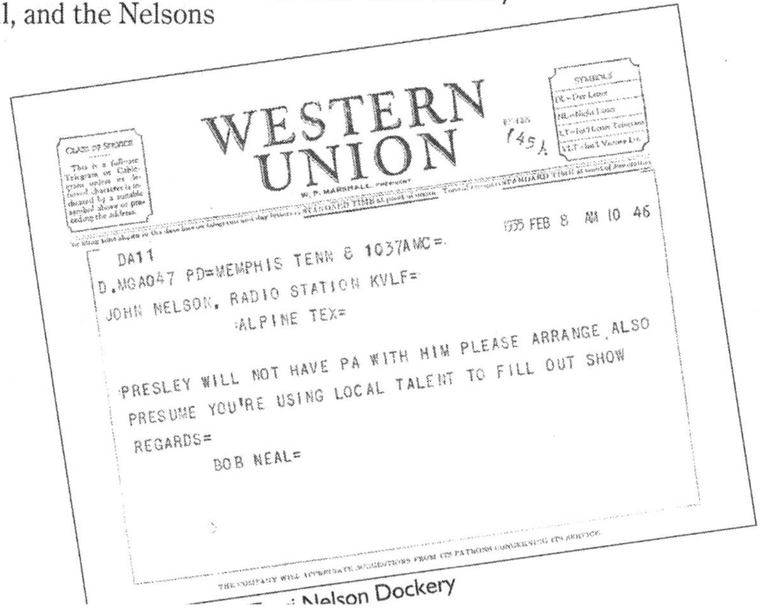
WESTERN UNION

W. P. MARSHALL, PRESIDENT

1955 FEB 8 AM 10 46

DA11
D.MGA047 PD=MEMPHIS TENN 8 1037AMC=
JOHN NELSON, RADIO STATION KVLF=
ALPINE TEX=

PRESLEY WILL NOT HAVE PA WITH HIM PLEASE ARRANGE ALSO PRESUME YOU'RE USING LOCAL TALENT TO FILL OUT SHOW REGARDS=
BOB NEAL=

Nelson Dockery

asked if he wanted to join them at a party at a fellow DJ's house. Elvis declined with a smile, glancing over to the corner where the banker's daughter loitered. He had a date. The girl admired her petticoat and smiled back at him appreciatively.

The next morning came very early to the boys. They staggered out of their rooms at the Bien Venido Motel on the main drag through town and stumbled over to the radio station for an interview and last minute automobile arrangements. They had to figure out how to get their limping car to New Mexico. A man by the name of Colonel Tom Parker booked the musicians for a gig in Carlsbad as a "favor" to Bob Neal. This would be the first but definitely not the last "favor" Parker performed for the boys.

Elvis Presley, Of Famed Louisiana Hayride, To Perform Here Feb. 10

Elvis Presley, the 20-year-old fireball from the Louisiana Hayride, will make a personal appearance in the Alpine High School Auditorium at 8 p.m. Thursday, Feb. 10.

The program is being held for the benefit of the Alpine High School FFA chapter. Tickets are now on sale.

Presley, along with his musical sidekicks, Scotty Moore and Bill Black, came upon his career quite by accident when a recording manager heard him making a personal record, and was so impressed that he signed him up to make records. The phenomenal success of "That's All Right Mama" and "Blue Moon of Kentucky" started a series of hits including "I Don't Care If the Sun Don't Shine", "Good Rockin' Tonight" and his latest release, "You're a Heartbreaker" b.w. "Milk Cow Blues Boogie." Elvis also does novel and rhythmic tunes on his shows that he has not recorded.

For a youngster catapulted from obscurity into a top starring spot on the big Louisiana Hayride show, Presley is remarkably pleasant and friendly, and always enjoys chatting with his many fans. He's single, and has no serious interests of heart — devoting what time he has to spare from his busy schedule of personal appearance — to working on his car, and indulging in his hobby of collecting pink and black clothes.

Scotty Moore plays the hot guitar, and Bill Black thumps the bass, and sometimes enjoys telling a few yarns on the other boys on the shows.

- Alpine Avalanche

The Bien Venido (Good Night) Motel

New Benefactors

February 13, 1955 - Lubbock - Fair Park Coliseum (afternoon)
February 13, 1955 - Lubbock - Cotton Club (evening)

If good luck shined on a musician in the eighteenth or nineteenth century, he might enjoy a royal patronage. For relatively decent money, the entertainer would play command performances every month or so to an adoring benefactor and the enthusiastic audience, who applauded loudly so as not to lose their heads. If such a thing existed in the fifties, then the Lowes of Lubbock might qualify, sans the missing head part. Just off old Slayton Highway, the Cotton Club booked the best musical talent to waltz through West Texas, from Bob Wills to Harry James. But for their favorite guest, the quiet-spoken boy from Tupelo, the Lowes bumped other singers off the bill to empty a spot for him.

Elvis first played the Cotton Club a few days after the new year. Despite the pitiful turnout, the Lowes took to the Hayride singer and invited him back for a February 13

Lubbock, Fair Park Coliseum. Courtesy of I. G. Holmes

performance, immediately following his appearance at the Lubbock Fair Park Coliseum. The twenty-five people who heard the young singer at the January program apparently ran home and told two friends, who told two friends, and so on, and so on, because the Cotton Club bulged with attendees in February, as it did every other time thereafter.

Impressed with the young man's politeness, Rob Lowe Senior would have booked Elvis again anyway, but of course, the money didn't hurt. Mrs. Lowe thought he was as cute as a bug's ear and wanted to collect him. The Lowe children remained skeptical.

Already disillusioned by the host of celebrities she'd met at her parents' club, the eight-going-on-thirty-year-old Pat couldn't give a rat's fuzzy behind who the man with the greasy hair and dandruff was.

Can I get down now? Pat Lowe and company at the Cotton Club, Lubbock 1955. Courtesy of I. G. Holmes

Would you like to meet Elvis? her mother asked excitedly.

No, she answered with the brutal honesty that only comes from children.

Elvis laughed. Oh, come over here and take a picture with me. He grabbed her in a brotherly noogie-hold and hoisted her onto a chair. After Elvis flashed a Pepsodent smile sure to win over the most stubborn female, Pat rolled her eyes but grudgingly permitted herself to be photographed.

Three-year-old Rob Lowe Junior needed no such convincing. After looking Elvis up and down, Rob Jr. readily accepted a new playmate, even if a very tall one. The two jammed together when the singer came to town—Elvis on his guitar, Rob on his ukulele. Once Rob Jr. became assured of the singer's musical ability, he allowed Elvis to invite him onto the Cotton Club stage one night, where they played a rock-a-billy concerto duet for guitar and uke. Sadly, the hit duo never cut a record together.

They did, however, swash a buckle through the tic-tac-toe world. One evening before a show, Rob Senior stormed upon the miscreants, Pat, Rob, and Elvis, who had just scribbled a fresh tic-tac-toe board on the dining room tablecloth. Guiltily Elvis slunk off to the show. The next day when the dry cleaners told Rob Sr. that they would charge him $1.50 to clean the tablecloth, he promptly threw the offending linen away. Less than half a year later, he regretted the hasty move.

Elvis reappeared at the Cotton Club in April and periodically through 1955 until his popularity grew so large that it actually became dangerous to play such a small venue. Lubbock locals were left with fond memories of a time when he was just their guy, and the secret about an incident in which some fellows attacked him after a Fair Park show and he kicked their collective butts back to Tupelo. Folks in the know shared the details the next day at Lee's Malt Bar and Grill, but not a whisper escaped its doors.

Elvis kept in touch with the Lowes over the years, including Pat, who staged teen rebellions by sneaking boys in the back door of the Cotton Club. One rascal who sweet-talked his way inside was the local geek, Buddy Holly. It seems he had some sort of passing interest in music.

Those session players are getting younger and younger. Buckaroo Rob Lowe Jr. rocks with the Man, Lubbock 1955. Courtesy of Rob Lowe Jr.

The Ol' Boys Network in Action

February 15, 1955 - Abilene - Fair Park Auditorium

Innocent of the wolves in Dacron suits following him, in December 1954 Elvis tooled over to Texarkana to play the Municipal Auditorium. As usual, he stopped at the local radio station the day of the show to do a promo piece. DJ Ernest Hackworth, affectionately known to his listening audience as Uncle Dudley, became intrigued with the strange, quiet-spoken young man completely at odds with the frenzied wildcat he had just seen on the Hayride stage. Alerted by the audience reaction to the singer, especially the female sector of the audience, Hackworth 'taught he 'taw a 'puddy 'tat. He took it upon himself to contrive a little test-gig for the boy. With a 500-seat capacity, the New Boston High School Auditorium served as the perfect lab. On January 9 while the Hillbilly Cat sang to Jo Hawkes and the other sighing sirens, Hackworth coolly appraised the new talent and congratulated himself.

A few days later Hackworth phoned his old friend and contact, Colonel Tom Parker. During the forties Parker owned Eddie Arnold of "The Cattle Call" fame, until an alleged dispute over Arnold's film career ended their relationship. At the beginning of 1955, Parker invested in Hank Snow, the country demigod. Hackworth suggested that it might be in Parker's best interest to check out some fresh blood he'd spotted at the Hayride. But hey, don't take my word for it, he said. Check out *Billboard's* recent rave about the young man's rendition of "The Milk Cow Blues Boogie" by K. Arnold. "Presley continues to impress," the magazine expounded with

Starlight, star bright, first star I see tonight . . . E. at the Hayride, Shreveport 1955. Courtesy of Pat Green

certainty.

Parker called Bob Neal, Elvis's newly appointed manager. Neal and Parker were old sparring partners; the unspoken truth looming between them was that Parker maintained much more extensive connections in the music industry. Parker booked better tours for his buds, with a substantial cut for himself, of course. Neal invited him out to the Louisiana Hayride to take a look at his fledgling singer, and Parker took him up on that offer. In January Parker went window shopping for talent in Shreveport. One look told him that Hackworth didn't exaggerate; the kid had definite possibilities.

Back in the office, Parker returned Neal's call. I've got a contact in Carlsbad, New Mexico, he told the man. Let's book the kid for the show, then send him on a little tour of West Texas with my boy, Hank Snow. They agreed on a date. Hank Snow was not consulted.

On February 13 Elvis began a five-day swing around West Texas starting in Lubbock. The bill included perennial favorite Slim Willet, Jamboree hot potato Charlene Arthur, and of course, Hank Snow, whom even the most tone-deaf homebody would travel miles to see. One thing about Parker, he delivered. Elvis suddenly revolved in higher circles.

When Elvis melted the Lubbock auditorium stage that night, Slim Willet—singer, songwriter of the Perry Como croon, "Don't Let the Stars Get in Your Eyes," and Abilene DJ—watched from backstage. After observing in amusement the extreme audience reaction to the newcomer, Willet called his fellow DJ friend Sid Foster in Breckenridge. Sid my man, you've got to see this guy, no kidding. And my advice to you is don't bring a date if you want to keep her.

Interestingly enough, Hank's son, the "— and Jimmie Rodgers Snow" decorating the bottom of the bill, developed an affinity for Elvis during their tour. Despite his father's travails, Jimmie later played backup for the Hillbilly Cat.

Intrigued, Sid Foster graced the audience at the Fair Park Auditorium in Abilene for the February 15 concert. The other performers excelled as usual, but when Elvis walked onto the stage, electricity flashed through the crowd, as if all the others had just been a warm-up. The singer, decked in brazen pink and black, opened his mouth as if he were about to sing but changed his mind and flashed a devilish grin. Next to Sid, a young girl keeled over in a dead faint on the floor. Sid thought to himself, oh man, I need to get this guy to Breckenridge.

After the show Sid searched backstage for Elvis, spotting him exiting the back door. As the cool night air rushed in, Sid tried to capture the attention of the man, but something more powerful held Elvis enthralled; a mighty hoard of trembling prepubescents rushed the entertainer. Panicking, Elvis fled to a nearby telephone booth and barricaded the door. Throbbing with hormones, the girls trapped him inside. When it became apparent that they weren't going to leave, Elvis bravely decided to face his peril. Cautiously he slid open the door and instructed all the girls to form a cadet line. After they came to attention, he signed their autographs and kissed each one in turn. Just when the first recruits darted to the end of the line for a second helping, his getaway car pulled up. Elvis jumped in and made his escape.

Unobserved, Sid Foster bust a gut laughing at the spectacle. Oh yeah, he definitely had to get this kid to Breckenridge.

An interesting historical side note to ponder: When Parker assumed Elvis's contract the following year, he offered Hackworth ten percent of the contract as sort of a finders fee. Hackworth didn't have the up-front capital at the time, so he passed on the offer.

In February 1955 -
First Secretary Nikita Sergeyevich Khrushchev demoted Premier Malenkov, removed Marshal Zhukov as Minister of Defense, and downsized Nikolai Bulganin to dogcatcher on his way to the top. By March 1958 he succeeded Lenin and Stalin as Russia's third absolute dictator since the 1917 Revolution.

First-term Senator John F. Kennedy underwent his second back operation and spent his recovery time writing *Profiles in Courage*, which became a best seller and won a Pulitzer Prize for biography.

No Need to Be Coy, Roy

February 16, 1955 - Odessa - Senior High School Field House

Slim Willet had spied on him two nights before in Lubbock, Sid Foster the next night in Abilene, and now four days into the tour (with one day off for good behavior), Roy Orbison studied Elvis from the front row of the senior high field house in Odessa. It's a wonder Elvis didn't seek psychotherapy for paranoid delusions.

The fifteen-year-old Texas boy watched Elvis onstage, looking for showmanship pointers he could use with his own group, the Westerneers. Halfway through the controlled frenzy of Elvis's performance, Roy decided he didn't have the stamina. "I never saw a guy with so much energy," Roy would tell people later in awe. The teenager became an instant Elvis aficionado, interviewing him excitedly for the radio station. Sadly, this tape like so many others was subsequently destroyed.

In the sixties Elvis returned the backhanded compliment. Long after Roy Orbison became a household name in the songwriting world, Elvis recorded Roy's "Running Scared." Disappointed with his own rendition, Elvis never released the record because he believed he didn't do justice to the song's illustrious writer.

Odessa High School Auditorium

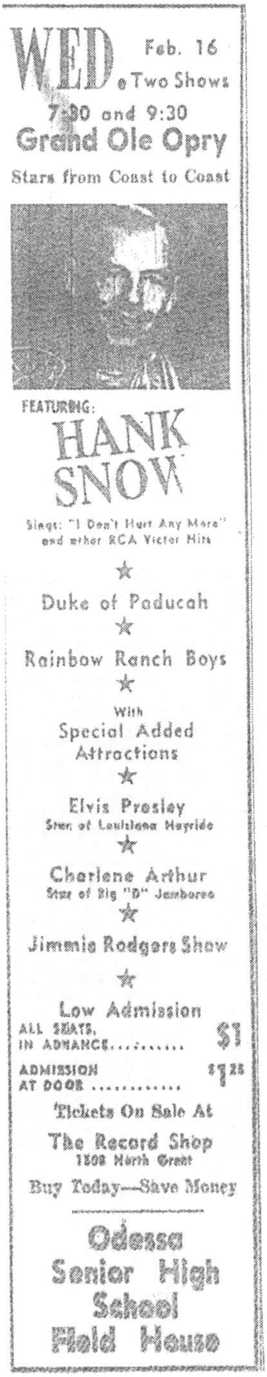

WED. Feb. 16
Two Shows
7:30 and 9:30
Grand Ole Opry
Stars from Coast to Coast

FEATURING:
HANK SNOW
Sings: "I Don't Hurt Any More" and other RCA Victor Hits
★
Duke of Paducah
★
Rainbow Ranch Boys
★
With
Special Added Attractions
★
Elvis Presley
Star of Louisiana Hayride
★
Charlene Arthur
Star of Big "D" Jamboree
★
Jimmie Rodgers Show
★
Low Admission
ALL SEATS, IN ADVANCE........ $1
ADMISSION AT DOOR $1.25
Tickets On Sale At
The Record Shop
1308 North Grant
Buy Today—Save Money

Odessa Senior High School Field House

Roy Orbison and Charlene Arthur. Courtesy of David Denard

Fit to Be Bow-Tied

February 25, 1955 - Texarkana - Municipal Auditorium

Just south of Texarkana and perfectly placed for three hungry singers to stop on the way to and from Shreveport sat Atlanta, Texas, home of the greatest little barbecue pit in the state. At least that's what Elvis, Scotty, and Bill thought when they stopped at three in the morning and the owners drug themselves out of bed to crank the oven.

In February 1955 the three weary travelers hit the rib joint during the day on their way to the Texarkana show. True, barbecue, like pancakes, really tastes best after midnight, but they had seven whole days to last before returning to their next Texas gig, so they crammed their faces with beef ribs, coleslaw, and pinto beans enough to properly fortify themselves for the rest of the drive and to carry them through any impending brisket-less days outside Texas.

Texarkana always gave Elvis a warm reception, even before they'd ever heard of him. But now, after several months on the Louisiana Hayride and his recent New Boston appearance, Texans flocked to the border town to see the man people called the Hillbilly Cat.

Ready for a good concert, the crowd had already started to party before Elvis showed his face. They sat poised for a dance tune and on cue, their boy delivered. When he swayed, they sighed. When he jerked, they jiggled and jumped. When he started his pelvic crunches, they screamed their endorsement

He seemed so sweet and wholesome, until the clothing started flying. Texarkana 1955. Courtesy of Marileon Hopkins Jerden

of his exercise regime. Caught up in the moment, Elvis tore off his bow tie and flung it into the crowd like a Chippendale's stripper. The ensuing scuffle and victory dance over the accessory didn't interrupt one note of the song, even though Bill Black was laughing so hard he could barely pluck the bass from his slumped position.

After the set, girls swarmed backstage to see if he had any other articles of clothing with which he would be willing to part. Disappointed, they had to satisfy themselves with an autographed picture. One brazen dame demurred so sweetly, that Elvis seductively unfastened his buttons and shed his shirt, handing the prize over to the astonished but instantly envied recipient. Not satisfied with the shirt off his back, she made him sign it.

The spontaneous bow tie gambit proved such a success in Texarkana that Elvis repeated the gesture in future concerts. To keep up with the demand, he bought a box of bow ties at his favorite clothing store in Memphis and hired a West Texas girl to sign his name on them. Her payment was a kiss and a bow tie, authentically signed, you can be sure.

Backing up from the microphone, E. gets ready to "do the dirty." Texarkana 1955. Courtesy of Marileon Hopkins Jerden

Punches for Presley

March 4, 1955 - DeKalb - High School Gymnasium

Ever since DJ Ernest Hackworth (a.k.a. Uncle Dudley) had interviewed Elvis for that December '54 Texarkana show, he'd kept his eyes and ears peeled for any decent money-making opportunities to waltz through his neck of the woods. He liked that quiet-spoken young man, and he thought Elvis had the correct fuel mixture to blast into orbit but just needed the right launch pad to combust upon.

So when the Lion's Club of DeKalb, a little town 30 minutes west of Texarkana, announced that it sought a vehicle to dig up a little capital for their cause, Hackworth knew just what to suggest. How about a benefit concert? he asked them. And he knew just the perfect person to pack the house... Señor Presley.

As the self-designated revenue-acquirers for the town's Lion's Club, the DeKalb football team thought the idea positively sparkled with its sheer brilliance. Many of them listened faithfully to the Louisiana Hayride broadcasts; several of the players even caught the January 9th New Boston show a few miles down the road. They thought that Elvis would surely be the easiest sale in the world, and in their impromptu poll, three-quarters of the seniors said they'd attend in a heartbeat ... and bring a date. That already added up to more return than their last two fund raisers combined. The DeKalb football team took a vote and announced that they endorsed the idea 100 percent. Their coach did not.

One day as various members of the team lounged around the locker room organizing the upcoming ticket sales attack, the coach poked his head out of his office and sauntered over to the huddle. He had made a decision, Coach told them. He didn't want his players helping sell tickets for that sex maniac. In the silence that ensued the members looked at each other to determine who would be

DeKalb Gymnasium

the first to laugh at what could only be a bad joke. Morris Hodgson drew the short straw.

He stood and adjusted his 6 foot 2 linebacker's frame so that the 747 wingspan he called shoulders would clear the overhead beams. Hodgson inquired politely, I beg your pardon, sir? (That's East Texan for "huh?")

Coach repeated himself to much the same reaction.

Trained since in vitro to speak respectfully to elders, Hodgson attempted to correct his coach's errant judgment. Elvis isn't a sex maniac, he told the coach, he's just . . . modern. Anyway, the kids love him and they'll pay to see him and that is after all, the point of a benefit concert (. . . and if you weren't a closet Boone collector, you'd understand this very elementary concept). Even though the last part of that sentence never actually left the linebacker's mouth, the coach must have heard it telepathically, because a shouting match ensued, followed shortly by a rush of testosterone that permeated the already saturated locker room.

In the left corner, at his first exhibition game, weighing 230 pounds, it's an incensed linebacker on a charitable mission. And in the other corner, returning to the ring after a ten-year Twinkie hiatus, we have a 240-pound self-righteous football coach. May the best ego win. Ding ding.

Both men circled each other, analyzing their opponent. Hodgson feinted with a spray of politically correct rhetoric; helping the Lions, feeding the starving orphans, that sort of thing. Suddenly Coach jabbed with an age discrimination barb and Hodgson was forced on the ropes flinging one of his own. Coach sucker punched with a sex-maniac insinuation, but before the referee could break the clinch, Hodgson retaliated with a clean right hook about middle-aged coaches and their alleged inability to recognize sex when they saw it.

Coach grabbed Hodgson (which was probably not the brightest thing to do to an angry linebacker), and Hodgson automatically punched back. The coach flew backward and de-racked a set of barbells.

At the inquiry, in front of Principal J. D. Loggins, fighting your coach over a rock 'n roll singer seemed much stupider in hindsight than it had during the heat of the battle. After much discussion, the principal gave his blessing to the ticket sales, but nixed any idea of a Hodgson/Coach rematch.

On the night of the concert, Hodgson manned the ticket table at the front door, mumbling under his breath that for all the trauma and his near expulsion, this concert better drive in bus loads of cash for the blankety-blank Lions, charitable or otherwise.

He didn't have long to grumble; tickets sold briskly and the house bulged with breathing-room-only space. Perky Betty Amos, sans the Carlisles, started the evening with a hopping tune, Scotty, Bill, and Jimmy Day pivoting to

Remember when...

school students pledged their allegiance to a flag with 48 stars? Alaska and Hawaii didn't become states until 1959.

Betty Amos belts out a tune with Jimmy Day (left) on the horizontal steel guitar and Bill Black (right) on the bass. Steel guitars appeared commonly in country western sets, but nearly became extinct when rock-a-billy metamorphosed into rock 'n roll. DeKalb, March 1955. Courtesy of Willie Cox

Hanging out in the locker room, DeKalb, March 1955. Courtesy of Willie Cox

the beat behind her. After touring East Texas with the Browns, Betty had agreed to a cameo for her old pal Elvis.

Meanwhile, Elvis surreptitiously snuck into the high school, friend Cheesie Nelson in tow. Cheesie detached and elbowed his way through the crowd to grab a good spot for the show, while Elvis detoured to the men's locker room, oblivious to the dislodged barbells and the reason for it.

Elvis prepared for the show, his attention distracted by Betty Amos cranking the crowd out on the floor. Normally he spent this portion of the evening pacing like a caged tiger, waiting for his turn to light the room, but his reverie was broken by Willie Cox, the local shutterbug. Toting his Argus c-3.35 millimeter camera, Willie asked Elvis if he minded a few snaps. Elvis told him he didn't mind at all and inquired about the camera. Diverted by Willie's favorite subject, the two spent the pre-game gabbing about techno-gadgets, cars they'd like to own but didn't, girls they'd like to date but couldn't (Elvis's end of the

How about that high-tech amp holder? Jimmy Day (left), Scotty Moore, E., and Bill Black (right) give the Lions something to roar about. DeKalb, March 1955. Courtesy of Willie Cox

conversation fell a bit sparse here), and sports that neither men played but wanted to. Elvis watched them and Willie shot them.

Next door, the wall thumping ended and Betty queued her bud to make his appearance. Elvis said his temporary alohas and exited the locker room, joining Betty on stage. Willie followed him around for the rest of the evening, snapping pictures whenever he got a good angle, unintentionally establishing the first East Texas paparazzi. Unlike future photographers too numerous to mention in Elvis's career, Willie had the class to cease and desist when Elvis waylaid his date for the evening, Jo Ann Hawkes.

Footnote: Perhaps it should be mentioned, that although Morris Hodgson continued to tackle through college and listen to Elvis, he never again combined the two sports.

Longhorns then Aggies

March 19, 1955 - College Station - Texas A&M G. Rolle White Coliseum

G. Rolle White Coliseum in College Station

After a disappointing turnout at Austin's Dessau Hall two nights before, the boys cast their sights on College Station, Texas, home of Texas A&M, and future Heisman Trophy winner John David Crow, who had just joined the football team that year and looked rather promising.

With the Louisiana Hayride sponsoring the concert, Elvis found himself in august company. Among the likes of Lester Flatt and Earl Scruggs and Little Jimmie "May the Sweet Bird of Paradise Fly Up My Nose" Dickens, Elvis barely rated a fourth position on the handbill.

Elvis arrived at the G. Rolle White Coliseum on the Texas A&M campus in overdrive. He and the Blue Moon Boys promised a three-concert deal to Biff Collie, the prominent DJ in Houston who gave the group one of their first breaks. Eagles Hall expected them at 8 p.m., and Bryan/College Station lay northeast of Houston about one hour's drive for normal people. Elvis, Scotty, and Bill could do it in thirty-five minutes after the farmers relinquished the two-lane roads to the speed-aholics for the evening.

Elvis asked the promoters if they minded if he and the boys played early, much to the audible groans of the other singers. Billed fourth or not, no one wanted to perform after Elvis on these traveling Hayride shows. The audience often left after his stint. Perhaps they didn't want the mood spoiled. Increasingly, no one wanted to perform *before* Elvis either. Ever since Hawkins, the Hillbilly Cat attracted a large contingency of teenagers that followed him to any concert near them. Unfortunately, they didn't hide their impatience very well and rustled rudely while the earlier singers tried to play. They hadn't as of yet booed anyone off the stage. But that time wouldn't be long in coming.

Elvis, Scotty, and Bill did their usual three to five songs then hit the road for Houston. The next day Biff had them scheduled to play Magnolia Gardens in the afternoon with Cook's Hoedown Club at night and then home-again home-again jiggity-jig.

In March 1955 -
Charlie Parker played his last public appearance at Birdland. He suffered a fatal heart attack four days later while watching the Tommy Dorsey TV show in his patroness' hotel room in Manhattan.

Guitar Homicide

April 13, 1955 - Breckenridge - High School Auditorium

After a break Elvis, Scotty, and Bill started another set of back-to-back gigs across north central Texas, starting in Breckenridge. Poised on the brink of West Texas, Breckenridge lay in Tornado Alley, about 100 miles . . . from absolutely nothing. Immediately after the show, the boys would have to scoot 166 miles through the "lake district" to their Thursday Gainesville concert, only to back-track past Breckenridge to catch Friday night's double feature in Stamford. On these long drives, Scotty and Bill usually alternated at the wheel, not out of deference to their lead singer, but out of sheer self-preservation. With a country-driver certainty that any road they traveled would eventually get him to his destination, Elvis maintained a brilliance for getting lost. Earlier ventures found Scotty jolted awake in the wee hours of the morning by the uneven surface of an abandoned gravel road. When asked for a location update, Elvis contentedly announced that he didn't know, while continuing to rocket through country so remote, even the local road-runners had to consult their GPS compasses. It's said that when you see road signs printed in Spanish, you should start worrying. Thus, Elvis-the-driver got demoted to Elvis-the-passenger for the majority of their adventures, except when they needed speed. Then Elvis was their man. This agreement lasted until Elvis bought his first car, a 1951 Lincoln Cosmopolitan he was so attached to they had to pry him out with a crowbar.

Scotty pulled up short in front of Breckenridge High School. The dirt that had chased them across the state finally settled across the broad hood of the used pink and

Breckenridge High School

white Cadillac, stuffed to the gills with band equipment. Last month, after a valiant struggle, the Chevy Bellaire got called to a higher service . . . station.

True to his promise in Abilene, DJ Sid Foster brought Elvis and the gang to his hometown stomping ground. Sid personally arranged the concert, filling the bill with the local talent of DJ/singer Ben Hall; country singer Onie Wheeler; Dean Baird, who played with the Champs of "Tequila" fame; Weldon Myrick, whose steel guitar stylings can still be heard behind many other famous musicians; Gene Funderburk; and Sid himself. (Why should they have all the fun?)

Sid made sure the concert received a plug from every DJ who owed him a favor, which constituted most of the state. Packed to the rafters with rock-a-billy aficionados ready to par-tay, the house band found it an easy task warming up the audience. They were already stoked when Elvis and the Blue Moon Boys vaulted on the stage and set the high school ablaze. The girls shrieked their approval of

Dean Baird, Bill, and Jimmy Day on steel guitar, Cisco 1955

I'm a pickin' and I'm a grinnin'. The boys in Breckenridge 1955. Courtesy of Jay Thompson

everything that came from Elvis's mouth. He could have sung "Row, Row, Row Your Boat," and the females would still have screamed. And when he gave them the come-hither look and sang, "I'd rather see you dead, little girl, than to be with another man," the women climbed over the seats and their boyfriends' heads to rip the orange and black Ricky Ricardo jacket off his body.

Needless to say, the boyfriends ceased to be quite so thrilled at the evening's entertainment. Bill danced with his bass and slapped it in time to Scotty's mad guitar pounding. Strings flew off Elvis's guitar as he literally ripped the chords off his Martin. Warned by Sid that Elvis played the guitar like a ravenous wolf with a T-bone, the house band stayed out of the range of the Martin jerking violently on the neck strap. Elvis had been known during particularly happenin' moments to slam the instrument backwards so violently that it bashed into the gut of any unsuspecting band member who stood within ten feet behind him. Years later when a newspaper reporter remarked to Johnny Cash that he played the guitar hard, Cash exclaimed, I don't play hard. Now, Elvis, he played hard. He broke strings before he got started.

Tonight the only victim to his enthusiasm was the ~~six-string~~, ~~five-string~~, ~~four-string~~, three-string. Bill Black asked backup Gene Funderburk if Elvis could borrow his guitar while the other one went into outpatient surgery. Gene resisted the temptation to clutch it to his chest and take off for parts unknown. Like a parent watching his only daughter moving out of the house, Gene painfully handed over the precious instrument to the wild man. Ironically, Elvis treated it like Gene's daughter, stroking the strings gently instead of wrenching them off the neck. (It might even be said that the guitar smiled afterward, but that's

Scotty preferred clever fingering, while E. was partial to chord-ripping. Breckenridge 1955. Courtesy of Jay Thompson

E.'s guitars lived harder on the road than their owner. Constant rubbing against his sharp belt buckle shredded them into matchsticks. This beautiful hand tooled guitar actually managed to make it through most of the state.

Breckenridge 1955. Courtesy of Jay Thompson

another story.) After the performance, Elvis returned it to its grateful owner/father, not a scratch marring the surface.

During the photograph signings, Elvis found himself a date to take to the Dairy Mart for a burger and Coke. He returned a few hours later to catch Sid's wife, cousin, and Sid himself going out for a late bite at the Why Not Café. A second dinner? Why not.

One of the girls at the show walked home that night, proudly bearing a newly autographed Elvis picture. When she got ready to pay the baby-sitter, she realized she'd just spent her last available dollar on a picture of the King. Instead of waiting for a bank to open in the morning, or an ATM to be invented in forty years, the baby-sitter opted to take the picture instead. Even though she hadn't been to the concert, she thought the man in the photograph looked handsome. That photograph is now worth about $750, pretty much what one night of baby-sitting costs today.

The next morning Elvis left town with the Breckenridge paper under one orange sleeve (to match the pink slacks). The headline on the entertainment page exclaimed:

SOME BOYS WOULD LIKE PRIVATE MEETING: SINGER CAUSES GIRLS TO NEAR SWOON - NOT THE BOYS.

The article stated that the male population remained less than euphoric about their girlfriends climbing over them to get to the singer. They would like to take Elvis out back and let him know how they feel about the situation. Apparently that article really upset Elvis. He confessed to several people that he didn't understand why his actions caused such an equal and opposite reaction in the community.

In later years Sid Foster and Elvis became

Psst, look over here. Breckenridge 1955. Courtesy of Jay Thompson

No, over here. Breckenridge 1955. Courtesy of Jay Thompson

friends, crossing paths many times, including sponsoring the Hillbilly Cat for two well-received shows at the Breckenridge American Legion Hall. Eventually Sid moved on to KDAV in Lubbock, the influential station that spawned so many musical icons. In doing so, he joined an elite collection of DJs who spun discs at that station in their career, including Bill Mack, Jay Thompson, and Waylon Jennings.

In April 1955 -
The "father of relativity," Albert Einstein, died. As a strong supporter of Zionism, he was offered the presidency of the state of Israel when President Chaim Weizmann died in 1952, but he declined the position, insisting that he was not worthy of the honor.

Elvis Hits a Home Run, But the Spectators Are Snagging a Weenie

April 14, 1955 - Gainesville - Owl Park Baseball Field

When Joe Leonard, the owner of KGAF Radio and Lin Records, booked Elvis to play at the Gainesville Baseball Field, he didn't exactly have philanthropy in mind. Mr. Leonard wanted to promote his own singer, Frank Starr, and thought that hitching him to the Hillbilly Cat would act as good exposure to him.

Mr. Leonard executed the usual advertisements on the radio and newspaper. His promos adorned every telephone pole in town. He even ordered a 25-count box of Presley's records from Big State Distributors in Dallas to sell at the show so he wouldn't be accused of playing favorites when he whipped out the trailer full of Frank Starr's single.

Elvis, Scotty, and Bill drove the couple hundred miles from Breckenridge to Gainesville. They arrived in town revved from last night's performance, ready for their Gainesville stint. Unfortunately, Gainesville wasn't ready for them.

The boys zigged through town and rolled out into the sticks, where radio station KGAF perched in the cornfield. Elvis, clad in his orange and pink travel best, crawled out of the Cadi and stretched his back after the long drive. Scotty and Bill spilled out after him. Slicking back his hair and fluffing up his sideburns, Elvis approached the front door of the radio station just in time for the station's chief engineer to spot them coming up the walkway. He yelled into the other room, panic clearly audible in his voice. Someone better lock the door; there's some hoodlum-types outside!

The DJ swiveled to peer out the window. Oh, it's probably those guys who are going to play tonight.

The three wandered inside and acted so polite during

Lock the doors, we're being invaded. Radio KGAF in Gainesville

their interview that the engineer felt guilty for planning to bolt the door on them. No one in the station mentioned the "hoodlum" comment to the performers. After the interview, Elvis, Scotty, and Bill drove back to town. They checked into the Curtwood Motel to grab a couple of winks before that night's show.

Owl Park, Gainesville

For the show, a couple of flatbed trucks had been maneuvered onto the Owl Park baseball field, where hundreds of empty bleachers awaited the throngs of eager music lovers. As eight o'clock neared, a handful of folks trickled into the stadium. At showtime, less than 200 people peppered the stands.

Elvis leapt onto the flatbed and played his heart out just as he did in Breckenridge, but the audience response lacked the electricity that zapped the halls of the high school. After the show, folks filed out without a word, leaving two big boxes of unsold records collecting dust on the baseball grounds.

Elvis apologized to Mr. Leonard for not making any money for him. Tickets sales netted $300, of which Elvis, Scotty, and Bill received $270. Leonard tried to console the visibly upset young man that folks around there liked their country music a bit more conservative than he delivered. Leonard told them he personally liked their sound very much. Unappeased, Elvis promised Leonard that he would do a free show for him to make up for the fiscal disaster. Leonard agreed.

Scotty, Bill, and a couple of KGAF's DJs drove across the Oklahoma border that night to drown their sorrows in a pint at a rustic joint called the B-29. Elvis attended his usual date, drowning his sorrows in another, less alcoholic, method.

A year later Elvis spied Leonard at a disc jockey convention. He marched over to the owner and told him to set a date. I'll come do a show for free 'cause I hate people to lose money because of me. By this time Elvis made several thousand dollars a performance, so his offer set the standard for generosity. Parker decidedly had other plans. The Colonel had scissored the word "free" out of his personal dictionary long ago.

In April 1955 -
After a mass trial in 1954 of 1,830,000 school children, Jonas Salk's polio vaccine was pronounced safe and effective. Salk received a Congressional Gold Medal and a Presidential citation from Eisenhower but refused financial compensation.

To Protect Her Name

April 15, 1955 - Stamford - High School and Roundup Hall 7 and 9 p.m.

Stamford High School

Judy Metz Jackson and Susan Ann McKnight grew bored watching the Stamford High School's April track meet, so they decided to leave and grab a Coke at the Super Dog in town. When they arrived, the two girls were stopped short by the vision of a pink and white Cadillac, parked like an alien spacecraft outside the dog stand. Curious if these were the Louisiana Hayride singers who were slated to play the high school gym that night, they forgot their weenie fix and followed the strange car to the local radio station, located like most of its kind, in the rural fields outside the city limits. One man hopped out of the car, and the two others sped off. The girls shimmied in the doors after their quarry. They scooted down the hall to their favorite DJ and barged in during an interview. The girls watched as the young man plugged his show that evening at the high school auditorium with a molasses-slow accent and invited folks to come out to the Roundup Hall afterwards. When the interview ended, the girls "hem-hemmed" their DJ until he introduced the handsome young stranger.

Apparently his name was Elvis Presley, and he didn't have a ride back to his motel. Would the girls do a big favor to the station and drive him back to town?

Oh, no problem absolutely, they just happened to be going that way.

Although the girls agreed on the transport, the seating arrangement caused a scuffle, which Elvis cured by sitting in the middle and putting his arm around each girl. He kidded with them all the way into town, and when they pulled up in front of his motel, he prodded Judy for a little kissy-poo goodbye.

I can't, I'm going steady, she quavered. (She'd even buckled the back of her hobble skirt so everyone would know her pre-premarital status.)

So am I, but who cares, Sue Ann replied, and Elvis gave her a tonsillectomy of a kiss.

Rumor spreads fast in small towns, but like the game of Operator, the truth got a bit distorted. By the dance at the Roundup Hall that night, everyone believed that *Judy* had been caught smooching with the musician, much to the girls' envy and her boyfriend's extreme annoyance. He made a scene on the dance floor. Elvis flew off the stage and told the boyfriend that Judy had turned him down because she was going steady with the boyfriend's worthless hide, not that he deserved her. Elvis didn't, however, bother to mention that Sue Ann apparently felt no conflict of interest.

Look, Elvis is a present.

In April 1955 -
After giving Great Britain her finest hour, Sir Winston Churchill resigns as prime minister. His protégé, Sir Anthony Eden, takes over.

To Protect Her Teeth

These auditorium bathrooms obviously weren't designed with rock singers in mind. Stamford Roundup Hall.

Apparently, April 15 was Damsels-In-Distress night at the Roundup Hall. Shirley Stewart drove from Abilene to attend the dance with her friends. None of them were on hand, however, when she got crushed by the surging crowd after leaving the poorly placed restroom. A wave shoved her petite frame into the stage at Elvis's feet and her teeth into the polished wood siding. After a few frantic seconds, she became airborne and landed on her feet facing Elvis, his hand under her arm. The show continued without a hitch, and after the set, Elvis found Shirley and asked her if she'd like to dance.

After touring the floor a few times, Shirley decided that he sure could sing, but he couldn't dance to save his ever-lovin' soul. A few bruised toes did not stop her, however, from accepting his generous invitation to drive her back to Abilene an hour away.

On the road to Abilene the two talked about his shows in the area and in particular, his performance in Breckenridge two nights before. Elvis pulled a newspaper clipping out of his wallet about the show. The journalist wrote that girls loved him, but boys wanted to take him out back, presumably to realign his facial features. Elvis told her that he didn't understand why those boys wanted to whip him; he was just trying to earn a living. He said he didn't want her to think he was bragging, but truthfully, he'd made more money at the show in Stamford than anywhere else before.

Shirley told him that speaking of earning a living, she and her friends had appeared on television that day modeling hairdos for the beauty school she attended.

Elvis told her, you may have beat me to TV, but I'll get there.

They arrived at the small apartment Shirley shared with her friends, and she invited him in. Elvis plopped onto the couch and propped his feet on the coffee table, and they gabbed for a while. Very shortly it became obvious that some of the girls had been preparing to go to bed. Elvis stood to leave. Shirley's roommate, Barbara, sauntered by on the way to her room and whispered coyly in her ear, make sure you get a kiss from him before he leaves. He must have overheard her, because just before leaving, Elvis remarked, you know, I like to treat a lady as I would expect someone to treat my sister, if I had one. With that, he bolted to Barbara's room and leapt onto her bed, trying to plant a kiss on her startled, shrieking lips, only to slide off her face. Good ole Golden Pencock Cream #1, face cream so greasy you can lube your car and your face at the same time. And oh yes, it protects you from rock singers with a sense of humor.

Big D is a Big Deal

April 16, 1955 - Dallas - Sportatorium

"Direct from Ed McLemore's Sportatorium in big D for Dallas, it's Saturday night country style!

Well, my goodness gracious sakes alive, it's another edition of Big D Jamboree brought to you direct from Dallas, Texas, home of us old hillbillies."

Owned by Ed McLemore and promoted by Ed Watt, the wrestling arena of the Big D Jamboree broadcast the movers and shakers of the hillbilly and rock-a-billy world across the airways of KRLD radio. For four hours straight, fresh young talent and a variety of emcees rotated onto the stage, a two-foot-high wrestling trampoline that had a tendency to bounce performers into the crowd when their gyrations became wild. The mish-mash of musical styles appealed to a wide audience and kept the barn dance venue kicking at a time when the standard country ditty began its slow slide

Johnny Cash. Sun promo photo from 1955

The Dallas Sportatorium, home of the Big D Jamboree, finally succumbed to real estate developers in 2001.

into an early demise.

With a keen eye for talent, Ed Watt lured relative unknowns like Johnny Cash and Carl Perkins to the arena, where the guests danced in the aisles and the shows were occasionally broadcast nationwide on CBS Radio. The list of artists who got their break on the Jamboree reads like a who's who of the recording industry:

- Johnny Cash
- The Carlisles
- Carl Perkins
- Hank Snow
- Tennessee Ernie Ford

Courtesy of Sid King

- Ray Price
- Hank Williams
- Sonny James
- Ferlin Huskey
- Slim Whitman
- Tex Ritter
- Wanda Jackson
- Sid King and the Five Strings
- Billy Walker "The Traveling Texan"
- Sherry Davis
- Marvin "Smokey" Montgomery and the Light Crust Doughboys
- and Charlene Arthur, a wild woman, from whom Elvis reputedly borrowed many of his stage moves.

One such nobody was Elvis Presley, whose original steal-of-a-price constantly increased over the five appearances he made. For Elvis's debut on April 16, Big State Distributors, the company who sold independent record labels like Atlantic and Sun to the jukebox operators, sent their heavy-hitter, Alta Hayes, out to make sure Presley didn't make a fool of himself on live radio. Convinced that Elvis would strike it big someday, Alta bought a couple hundred copies of "That's Alright, Mama" from Sun. To hedge her bets, she hired a gaggle of girls to sit in the front row of the arena and yell like they enjoyed the show when he played. She gave them records as bribery. Sure enough, when he appeared on stage, the girls started screaming and carrying on. It looked like Alta got her money's worth, but as Smokey Montgomery of the Light Crust Doughboys remarked later, those girls didn't scream any louder than the unpaid girls.

In June Elvis played under Marty Robbins, but by September he headlined.

Alta Hayes, Big State Distributor's Secret Weapon, 1955.
Courtesy of Tony Ventura

Betty Amos with the Carlisles, 1955.
Courtesy of Ms. Traci Nelson Dockery

Wanda Jackson

Charlene Arthur of the Big D Jamboree.
Courtesy of David Denard

Scotty, E., and Bill, jammin'. Big D Jamboree, Dallas 1955. Courtesy of David Denard

Remember when...

bowling lanes had human pinsetters? Hidden at the back of the alley, the setter dropped from his perch when the pins fell and replaced them to their starting position. Really modern joints had a rack to ensure exact placement, but older lanes relied on the tried-and-true foot pedal method that raised nails at the back of the alley to set the pins on.

That smoldering look. Scotty, "Uncle" Johnny Hicks (in background), E., and Bill on the wrestling trampoline at the Big D Jamboree. Courtesy of Steve Bonner and David Denard

Double Trouble

April 25, 1955 - Wichita Falls - M-B Corral
April 25, 1955 - Seymour - High School Auditorium

SEYMOUR IN PERSON - -
ELVIS PRESLEY
L.A. HAYRIDE SENSATION
WITH HIS BLUE MOON BOYS
SCOTTY AND BILL
THAT'S ALL RIGHT, MAMA
AND MANY MORE
DERREL DICKSON, CAPITOL
RECORDING ARTIST
MAMA LAID THE LAW DOWN
TO ME, PLUS TNT'S
NEWEST RECORDING ARTISTS
GENE KAY AND CHUCK LEE
ALONG WITH
WALKIN' "A" RANCH HANDS
BIG SHOW, LOTS OF LAUGHS
HIGH SCHOOL AUDITORIUM,
APRIL 25, 1955,
7:30 to 9:30

Pity that cloning hadn't already been invented in the fifties, because on the night of April 25, TNT Records in San Antonio booked Elvis and the Blue Moon Boys simultaneously in two different towns. The boys arrived at the M-B (Miller Brothers) Corral in Wichita Falls, only to find that the Seymour Volunteer Fire Department expected them to play at the Seymour high school auditorium as a desperately needed fund raiser for their town of 4,000. Already late for the start time in Seymour, Elvis ran up to the office of the Corral and called his mother for advice during the break at the Wichita Falls show. The local DJ and a couple of the Miller brothers accidentally eavesdropped on the distressed monologue. Apparently she advised him to fulfill both obligations, because Elvis hung up the phone and asked if the Millers could cover for them until they returned.

Forty-five minutes into the frantic drive to Seymour, the car coughed and crawled to a stop outside Mabelle. The gas gauge read "E" for "Ewe should have filled me up before you left." After a few head bangs, Scotty, Bill, and Elvis started thumbing. There's nothing quite like being stranded on a Texas road. Unlike other states where you might actually stumble upon another car

MON., APR. 25
TNT Records
Presents

Elvis Presley
" THAT'S ALL RIGHT MAMA "
" BLUE MOON OF
" KENTUCKY "
" GOOD ROCKIN' TONITE "
" HEART BREAKER "
M-B CORRAL
Shepperd Access Road
Phone 2-0101 3-5641
Available for Private Parties

within a few hours, in Texas it is entirely possible to drive ten hours and never catch even a whiff of exhaust fumes from another vehicle. Such was the case where our heroes broke down. In the pitch black of North Texas night, they stumbled over the mesquite shrubs and snoring rattlesnakes, vainly watching for telltale headlights to illuminate unbroken miles of desolation. Too bad AAA wasn't around yet. An unlimited towing package would have paid for itself in two months with these guys.

Fortunately for our brave lads, bouncing along the highway on their way home from the concert in Wichita Falls, a carload of teenagers spied a pink Cadillac on the side of the road. As one didn't commonly see Mary Kay cars lounging around on two-lane roads around this neck of the woods, it got their attention. At the M-B Corral, these kids had waited seemingly forever for Elvis and company to return to the stage, but after an hour of the Miller Brothers, they gave up and hightailed it home so the girls wouldn't miss their curfew. A few moments later the headlights pinned three familiar figures tripping over rocks a mile in the distance. The kids couldn't believe their luck. Hey, aren't those the guys from the show?

They stopped. After briefly discussing the situation, the girls piled on their

Seymour High School Auditorium

boyfriends' laps and they drove the oddly dressed hitchhikers into Seymour.

The volunteer firemen had been watching for the singers for some time now, seeing their hopes for a profitable show going down in flames, so to speak. Painfully late, Elvis, Scotty, and Bill arrived in front of the high school auditorium, where they crawled out and explained their situation to one of the firefighters stationed there. He volunteered to take the musicians back to their car with extra gas. As thanks for coming to their rescue, Elvis gave each of the teenagers an autographed picture and an invitation to watch backstage at the Seymour show, if he ever made it back there that night. The kids figured, two shows in one night... cool. They called their parents to see if somehow the curfew could get stretched a bit for a very worthy cause. The volunteer fire department was a bona fide charity, after all.

Elvis, Scotty, and Bill got back to their car, gassed her up, and returned to Seymour, the fireman tailing them just in case. By the time Elvis arrived at the high school auditorium, the natives had grown way past restless and moved directly into coup potential. "TNT's own" Gene Kay and Chuck Lee had already repeated their sets and were working on their third round, while desperately hoping no one in the brewing, growling mob carried any produce. The emcee appeared several times, reassuring the angry throng that Elvis had called and he was on his way, a boldface lie considering cell phones didn't adorn Cadillacs for another forty years. Many people who paid had to leave. They were replaced by folks off the street who wandered into the auditorium,

Seymour High School Auditorium, still showcasing new talent

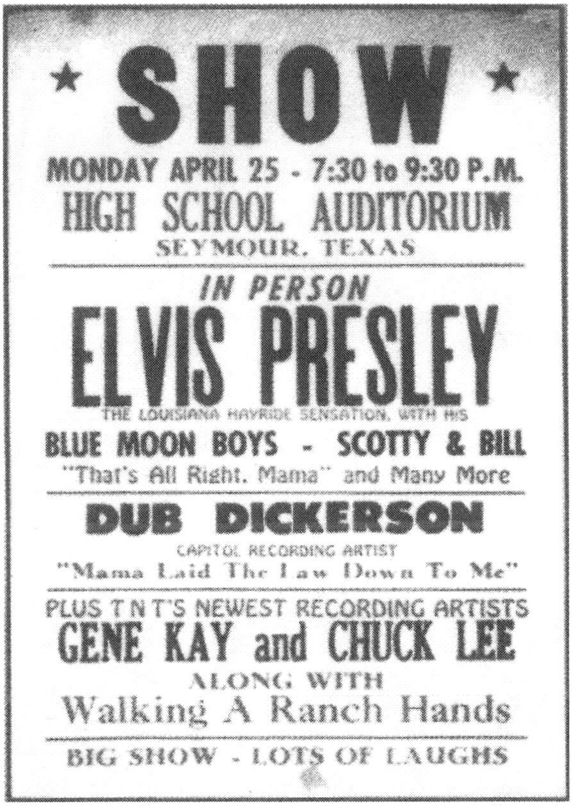

Courtesy of Dr. Dennis Hickey

lured by the smell of blood.

At 10:30 a girl in the auditorium screamed, He's here!

Scotty and Bill walked onstage. Scotty somberly stepped to the microphone and announced, sorry folks, Elvis couldn't make it.

The girl screamed again. He's here, I saw him come in.

Scotty laughed and plugged his guitar into the amp. Bill took his customary position on the right. Elvis landed on the stage wearing appropriately enough, a fire-engine red sport coat, white shirt, bow tie, and blue trousers two sizes too big, so he could perform his gyrations without ripping his pants. Guitar suspended in front of him, Elvis ambled to the microphone, tugged on his pants, and stood with half closed eyes. Scotty looked him over for a few moments and stepped behind the singer, pretending to wind him up. Leg shaking, Elvis launched into "That's Alright, Mama" and the show took off.

After five back-to-back numbers, Elvis spoke to the crowd. "Ladies and gentlemen, we aren't really supposed to be here tonight. We were booked into the M-B Corral over at Wichita Falls for a dance. We didn't know about this booking until we got a phone call earlier in the evening and found out about the mix-up. We weren't gonna come, but we found out all you folks were waiting for us, so we talked the Miller Brothers into letting us run over here for a little while. We were in such a hurry, we ran out of gas about twelve miles out of town and had to hitch a ride in. Hectic man. Anyway, we made it and we appreciate you waiting for us."

The band played for forty minutes to the delighted crowd. When Elvis wrapped up the show, fans rushed the stage seeking autographs and kisses. One girl leaped into his arms asking, Do you remember me?

Yes, I met you in Stamford.

Elvis never was one to forget a face, especially a female one.

Scotty and Bill packed the equipment in the car, and the three sped back to Wichita Falls, some of the teenagers trailing them to catch the show for the second and third time that night. When the trio arrived at the Corral, the carriage had already reverted into a pumpkin and the footman into a hound dog. Pal Billy Thompson and the Miller Brothers entertained the throng as they promised until Elvis returned, but much of the audience had already left the house, muttering darkly under their breath.

Elvis never accepted another booking from TNT Records again, partly because he didn't trust them, but mostly because they folded shop a few months later. Despite Elvis's Herculean attempt to play both places that evening, he managed to satisfy neither. Gene Wagner, one of the owners of the M-B Corral, remained furious that "that snotty-nosed kid" had returned to the Corral way too late. The promoters of the Seymour gig simply didn't pay him.

M-B Corral, Wichita Falls

Boy, am I glad to see you! Billy Thompson stalls for time, 1955

Get a Haircut!

April 26, 1955 - Big Spring - Municipal Auditorium

Scotty, Bill, and Elvis rolled into Big Spring with sleep on their mind. The previous night's double booking had kept them playing until the wee hours of the morning. They found a motel in Big Spring and crashed for a few hours.

Just before lunch, Elvis burned some of his restless energy by visiting the town's record shop, famous for both their selection of new releases and also for its eccentric owner, Oscar Glickman. Elvis spotted Glickman behind the register and after some introductions, tried to strike up a deal. Elvis had the back end of the car filled with boxes of records. He told Glickman he'd cut him a deal to carry them. Selling records out of the back of your car was standard operating procedure for smalltime recording artists in those days. Most musicians had to do a great deal of self-promotion to ever get heard.

Glickman hesitated. He didn't need another box of unsellable 78s cluttering up his store. Instead, he invited the kid to lunch at his favorite place around the corner. The restaurant was so small that if you wanted a table, you had to ask people to vacate the seats ...nicely of course. The two maneuvered into the narrow restaurant

Big Spring Municipal Auditorium

and picked out something delicious and thoroughly unwholesome to eat. Meanwhile, Glickman appraised Presley for sales profitability. Elvis chatted in such a self-effacing, charming manner that Glickman reluctantly agreed to buy a box of records.

You really need to change your style, Glickman told Presley as the young man scooped a box from the back of the car. You won't ever make the big time looking like that.

A few dollars richer, Elvis drove off to prepare for the evening's performance. Glickman put one record on the shelf and hauled the rest of the Sun label 78s to the basement, where forty years later, Glickman's grandson stumbled across them.

Today, many of the records are worth $250 each.

Big Spring Record Shop in its current disguise.

Cisco Kid Was a Friend of Mine

April 28, 1955 - Cisco - Community Hall

After selling those records in Big Spring, Elvis, Scotty, and Bill had arrived in town that afternoon with a few extra bucks burning a hole in their pockets. So they decided to partake in their favorite pastime, eating. The threesome rolled over to the White Elephant Café in next-door Eastland and snagged a booth in the back, scanning the female life forms for possible date prospects. When what to their wondrous eyes should appear, but Billie Garrett, daughter of a Texas oil man, sashaying in the door. They hadn't seen Billie since the Tyler show, so Scotty waved her over to join their progressive dinner club.

Upon paying the waitress, the boys discovered they still had a quarter or two left and decided they still had time to catch the cowboy flick playing at the downtown theater before their show that night. Twenty minutes into the film, the group acquired a serious case of B-movie giggles. The film was so awful that Elvis improved the dialog with a little of his own, more artistic stylings.

Hush your face. Billie Garrett and E. April 1955. Courtesy of Billie Garrett

Scotty and Bill rolled in their chairs, unable to suppress snorts of laughter, earning them dirty looks from their fellow patrons. Billie punched Elvis to make him shut up to no avail. When his comments teetered slightly into blue territory, Billie hissed at him to hush his face or they'd be kicked out by the ushers, a thought that only seemed to amuse him more. They managed to escape the movie before the credits rolled and the theater gestapo could arrest them for disturbing the peace.

Elvis and Scotty invited Billie to catch the show that night. She accepted, telling them she'd drag her great uncle and aunt with her. They could use a night out.

With the same precise planning that hallmarked the Seymour/Wichita Falls fiasco, TNT Records arranged the Cisco concert. They booked the hall and the band but forgot to invite the audience. When Elvis and the Blue Moon Boys arrived, only a handful of people stared disinterestedly back at them. Billie and her family's arrival nearly doubled the audience.

Hello, is anybody there? Cisco, April 1955.

Giving new meaning to the "warm-up session." Midland, May 1955.

Billie waited until the "crowd" subsided, then introduced her aunt and uncle to the boys. She told them how much she enjoyed the concert, and Elvis seemed to appreciate the gesture. Billie left them that night with a promise that she'd catch up with them whenever they played in a town near her. The following month she fulfilled her word by appearing at the KOCA Radio concert in Kilgore.

During the poorly attended show at the small baseball park near the high school, some particularly obnoxious teenage boys heckled the singers. Elvis responded to their slings and arrows with all the maturity and understanding his age would permit . . . he bent over and pointed his butt at them in mid-stanza.

Billie tracked her favorite singing group to a modest turnout for Midland in May, where she snapped a picture of him hanging out in the gym before the show. In August Billie convinced her father to see Elvis perform at the Reo Palm Isle in Longview. Although substantially more people turned out for this concert than the last time he played there, a majority of the 1,800 glitzy chairs still sat vacant.

After the show she introduced her father to the singer and held her breath. The oilman and Memphis boy faced off. When Elvis spoke, his southern, polite background always seeped through. He respectfully called everyone "sir" or "ma'am" and seemed genuinely interested in listening without judgment. He and Mr. Garrett liked each other immediately. They joked back and forth, her father tossing out questions just to see what the young man would say. Elvis good-naturedly answered each one, seemingly aware of the scrutiny. After about ten minutes, Billie remembered to breathe.

Halfway into the conversation, Mr. Garrett asked if Elvis gave autographs at these concerts. Elvis admitted he did sign photographs mostly, but occasionally other things.

Like, what other things? the oilman wanted to know.

One girl once wanted me to sign her petticoat, Elvis told him.

The oilman laughed and asked if he signed French cuffs.

Oh, absolutely, Elvis confirmed.

Mr. Garrett proffered his sleeve, and laughingly, the young man signed it. The oilman supervised the job to make sure Elvis spelled his own name correctly. Since the suggestion had only been a joke, her father threw the shirt out soon after.

You could have knocked Billie over with a feather when the following year the same soft-spoken young man who had nearly gotten them kicked out of the theater appeared on the big screen with Debra Paget. She had visited four or five of his shows during the year, and none of them pulled in more than 150 people . . . tops. He was always just one of the gang. How did this guy suddenly become so famous?

An Arresting Performance

April 30, 1955 - Gladewater - High School Gymnasium

Honey, you won't believe what just walked through my door! The owner of the Blue Grill Café eyed the threesome that entered just before closing time.

What is it, Mama?

Three of the most outlandish creatures I've ever seen, wearing clothes not fit for a dog-hanging. And one of 'em has sideburns down to his kneecaps.

I'll be right there.

Elvis, Scotty, and Bill hobbled tiredly into the restaurant. They'd just driven across the breadth of the state from Lubbock in far West Texas to Gladewater in East Texas. They looked famished and exhausted, and they smelled like they'd just traveled 430 miles on two-lane roads. Mrs. Landers led them to an isolated table.

Do you mind if I move the car around back? Elvis asked the owner. I want to keep an eye on the instruments.

Mrs. Landers nodded her approval and followed him out the door to satisfy her curiosity. She was not disappointed. The big pink car swelled with boxes, clothes, and unidentified shapes. A huge bass fiddle reclined on top, a hillbilly mobile if she'd ever seen one.

The Blue Grill, now serving good Texas cooking to strange men in pink cars.
Blue Grill, Gladewater, April 1955

Carol Landers came pelting around the corner in time to see the car pull behind the cafe. Her eyes grew very wide and she looked at her mother for explanation.

Musicians.

Oh!

The two ladies returned inside to take their guests' order. When Mrs. Landers entered the kitchen, Elvis stood propped against the counter talking to the cook, Clarence Cobb. Apparently Clarence played music himself, and they had a great deal in common. The two men chatted amiably for over an hour, Elvis never seeming to notice that his actions would be considered peculiar in the segregated South.

The concert that night starred the displaced Louisiana Hayride cast, headed by Slim "Indian Love Call" Whitman and including Johnny "First Train Heading South" Horton and Gentleman Jim "Mexican Joe" Reeves. Their standard auditorium in Shreveport bounced them for the yearly carnival, so the Hayride moved to the high school gymnasium in Gladewater, compliments of KSIJ Radio and DJ Tom Perryman. KSIJ already broadcast the Hayride on their station, so why not play it live from there as well?

Gladewater's Rich Fenton Gym

JC's Name Teams To Sell Hayride Advance Tickets

The Gladewater Junior Chamber of Commerce today named teams and captains in their ticket sales campaign for the Louisiana Hayride show which appears here Saturday night, April 30.

Chuck Miller, ticket chairman, said the JC's have approximately 2,500 tickets for sale. The show to appear here will make its regular Saturday night radio broadcast from the high school gymnasium in Gladewater. This is one of the few times which the Hayride has left its home base at Shreveport.

Admission prices are $1.00 for adults, 50 cents for children. Persons wishing to buy tickets may contact any of the following JC's listed below in teams:

- April 12, 1955, Gladewater Daily Mirror

Jaycees To End Ticket Selling

All Gladewater Jaycee members will turn in their tickets Friday for the Louisiana Hayride Show to be presented here Saturday night, it was announced today by ticket sale chairman Chuck Miller.

At present, about 1,300 tickets have been sold. Arrangements are being made to seat about 2,500.

Jaycees are asked to turn their tickets in Friday to either Miller or Don Smith.

Work details will be called at 7 p.m. on Wednesday, Thursday, and Friday, to get the gym ready for the show. A tar paper covering is to be placed on the gym floor to protect it from being scratched by chairs. Jaycees will lay this covering and set up the stage and other work necessary before the big 3½ hour show comes here.

The Hayride nationally known hillbilly radio show from radio station KWKH in Shreveport, La. will present its full Saturday night show from the Gladewater gym. The show will be broadcast over KWKH, and the regular half-hour CBS nationwide hookup will be broadcast from here also.

- April 26, 1955, Gladewater Daily Mirror

The Jaycees sponsored the show and copiously sold the tickets, stuffing 3,000 people into a 2,500 capacity hall and turning hundreds of procrastinators away at the door. Just before the first act captured the stage, master of ceremonies Horace Logan announced that their headliner, Slim Whitman, had taken ill.

We've got this new kid that's going to sing for you, named Elvis Presley, he told the disappointed audience. They didn't stay disappointed long. This was Elvis's night to sparkle. He dazzled the onlookers with his clothes, his moves, the Tony Curtis sneer he'd been perfecting in the mirror for months, and most

Gladewater High School Gym

especially, the music, which before seemed edgy and unpolished, now sounded wild and magical.

He set the stage on fire and incinerated the walls of the high school and the libidos of the young woman. Backstage, the girls swarmed around Elvis, their friendly pats and comradely hugs turning more provocative by the minute. They rubbed up against him, and Elvis responded playfully . . . too playfully, it seems, to suit the local police. They dragged Elvis away from the throng, warning him that if he didn't knock off the touchy-feely games with the underage girls, they would make sure he had a great deal of solitary time to rethink his participation. As our hero did not spend quality time at the Gladewater A-Rest-Mor motel, we can only assume that he wisely heeded the local authorities.

Here April 30

Cast Of 40 To Be On Hayride

A cast of over 40 hillbilly music performers will be present here Saturday night, April 30, when the well-known Louisiana Hayride comes to Gladewater with its 3½ hour radio program.

Ticket sales for the show are going fast, the club reports. Already over $600 in tickets has been sold.

The cast for the show here will include the following list of well-known artists: Elvis Pressley [*spelled wrong*] and band; Jim Reeves and band; Johnny Horton, Jimmy Newman and band, Billy Walker, Tibby Edwards, Bundy Attaway, Jack Ford, J. E. and Maxine Brown, Hoot and Curley, Betty Amos, Jeanette Hicks, Jimmy and Wayne, Floyd Cramer and Jimmy Day and band, and the Lump Lump boys.

Announcers will be Horace Logan, Frank Page and Norm Bale.

Elvis Presley, Sun Recording artist, and more than 40 nationally known folk music artists will appear with the Louisiana Hayride at the High School Gymnasium in Gladewater on April 30th. Elvis' unique style has earned him the title of "The Bopping Hillbilly." Certainly his arrangements are unusual and his two-piece band, SCOTTY and BILL has set an instrumental style that is being widely copied. Some of his recordings include "That's Alright," "Blue Moon of Kentucky," and his latest "You're a Heartbreaker." Elvis, Scotty and Bill live in Memphis, Tennessee.

- April 20, 1955, Gladewater Daily Mirror

Dallas Dealings

May 28, 1955 - Dallas - Sportatorium

Take your waitress by the waist and twirl her round without much haste. Swing her high, swing her low, but don't step on that pretty little toe. Sashay.
Linda Gray Arnold and E. at the Big D Jamboree, Dallas 1955.
Courtesy of Steve Bonner

Who in the hell is Orville Couch? He owes me a buck. The colorful language slipped uncustomarily off Elvis's palate as he stormed in the back door of the Big D Jamboree.

I'm Orville Couch, the country singer admitted, turning in his seat.

Elvis straddled a chair in front of the man. Two girls outside the door made me join your fan club, he declared in outrage.

Orville sputtered with laughter. Mood broken, the two men chatted until the emcee cued them. The two singers shared much in common. Both crossed the thin line between hillbilly and rock, but unlike Elvis, Orville preferred to stay to the country side of the road. Elvis never did get that dollar back, but at least he could whip out his Official Orville Couch Fan Club Lifetime Membership card if the circumstances ever called for it.

On May 28 Ed Watt of the Big D Jamboree booked Elvis to play Dallas again for the second time in as many months. Just as before, Elvis "paid his dues" when he rolled into town and visited Big State Distributors on 137 Glass Street, in what the locals now call the textile district of Dallas.

In the fifties the Big Three: RCA, Decca, and Columbia attended to their own record distribution, as well as a young upstart called Capitol Records. The smaller labels and independents relied on Big State Distributors to push their 45s to the jukebox owners. As Big State maintained total discretion with regard to what records to ship, it paid a newcomer to do a little promo work while in town.

Elvis wandered in and checked on sales, signed the occasional autograph on record sleeve, scrap paper, used lunch sack, whatever made the boys with the paychecks happy. Very happy indeed they became when Elvis's records flew off the store shelves in the months that followed. They congratulated themselves on their excellent promotional skills, gave Alta Hayes, Elvis's company benefactor, a raise, and toasted each other with well-earned champagne ... right up to November 20. In an attempt to promote Jerry Lee Lewis and Carl Perkins, Sam Phillips of Sun Records signed all of Elvis's catalog rights over to RCA, lock, stock and barrel. Big State's first round draft pick got traded under the table to the Redskins. Almost overnight they faced their star in the enemy lineup.

Digging up some business at Big State Distributors. Dallas 1955

You Know That I'll Always Be Lovin' You

May 31, 1955 - Odessa - Senior High School Field House

When Carolyn Bradshaw joined the Louisiana Hayride in 1954, her mother warned her against the instability of musicians, but the seventeen-year-old headstrong girl felt safe within the family atmosphere of the Hayride and the protective influence of Floyd Cramer and Jimmy Day. She spread her musical wings and earned a hit with her record, "The Marriage of Mexican Joe," an answer to Jim Reeves' top ten "Mexican Joe."

In 1954 she took a three-month leave of absence to replace a pregnant singer at the Cliffie Stone Hometown Jamboree in California. She returned in November to find the Hayride aflutter.

Did you see the new guy, Elvis Presley, yet? The women asked her.

No, why?

You'll see, they warned her. And she did.

Elvis walked in the door and their eyes met. He gave her a just-arrived-and-still-

Carolyn Bradshaw and E. at the Hayride. Shreveport 1955.
Courtesy of Bobby Holeman

vulnerable smile. Suddenly she understood all the fuss the women made over him. Elvis worked fast, and by the December show in Hawkins, they were dating steadily.

When they played the Hayride, Elvis picked her up for a date afterwards in Jim Ed Brown's father's Chevy. They cruised Shreveport's burger spots and gabbed, their conversations growing more personal over the months, until one evening Elvis confided that he felt guilty that he had lived and his twin brother had died at birth. Sometimes when they caught a movie, Elvis had anxiety attacks and would stand and sit and stand and sit until Carolyn dragged him out of the theater for a walk. He prowled the streets with her, full of restless energy.

When the group traveled to shows in Texas, Louisiana, or Arkansas, Elvis and Carolyn sat in the back of Scotty's Chevy and sang old-time-religion spirituals at the top of their lungs. Bill and Scotty sat up front, grimacing and plugging their ears.

As the months rolled through 1955, Elvis spent more time on the road with Scotty and Bill and less with her. Weeks would pass between the times she saw him. Each time, he returned, weary from the road but considerate as always. When Elvis invited his parents to the Hayride, he introduced them excitedly to Carolyn, like she was his favorite school playmate. His mother, Gladys, shook her hand like a doe caught in the headlights and stayed close to her son's side as if the other singers might eat her. Vernon shook her hand absently, staring around the stage in country-boy awe. She realized Elvis must never have mentioned her name to his parents, because they looked at her blankly when he introduced her. That seemed a very bad omen for the future of their romantic involvement.

In May Carolyn played a concert in Odessa with Johnny Horton. When the curtain opened, six people stared back at them from the expanse of the auditorium. The rest of the crowd screeched nearby at the Elvis concert. She, Johnny, and the rest of the cast gave the six lost souls their money back and with an "if you can't beat 'em, join 'em" attitude, drove over to the high school field house to see the Hillbilly Cat themselves. They headed around to the backstage door and stopped in their tracks. Four hundred girls swarmed Elvis, trapping him against the exit door and preventing him from escaping. She and Johnny

Remember when...

Danny Thomas was the perfect daddy, Eve Arden was the perfect teacher, and Groucho Marx was the perfect game show host?

attempted to catch his attention, but to no avail. A pink Cadillac moved through the crowd unobserved. A few moments and a couple hundred autographs later, Elvis slipped back inside the door. While the fans stood around waiting for his reappearance, Elvis shimmied out a window on the other side of the building and dropped onto the roof of the getaway car below.

In a painful revelation, Carolyn admitted to herself that Elvis must have been seeing other girls on the road while dating her. Pappy Covington of the Hayride took her aside and put a fatherly arm around her shoulders. Honey, you really don't believe Elvis could be with only one girl, do you? he asked.

Carolyn ripped up the picture Elvis autographed especially for her and cried her eyes out.

If I'm seen with someone new, don't be blue. I'll be faithful, I'll be true, always true, true to you.

– E. Presley, "Lovin' You"

April Showers Bring May Glowers

April's performance in Gladewater ended the uncertain month on a bang, and the beginning of May seemed so very promising. But life on the road began to grow old. In the middle of May, 14,000 fans showed up at a baseball park in Jacksonville, Florida, and tried to devour Elvis in their excitement. He joked with them that he'd see them backstage after the performance, and they obliged. Thousands of them chased him into the shower and stole his clothing. But when he played at the KOCA radio baseball field in Kilgore after a month's hiatus from Texas, the stands remained nearly vacant, except for those who came for the hot dogs.

On May 25 Elvis was invited to appear in a parade during the Jimmie "Honeycomb" Rodgers Memorial Celebration in Meridian Mississippi, but the crowds booed him for his corruption of their favorite music style. Hank Snow and Colonel Tom Parker fought over the attention Elvis pulled away from the show regulars, Parker and Neal fought over Neal's ability to promote Elvis in the big leagues, Elvis became frustrated with the no-shows back to back with concerts like Florida, and Scotty and Bill snarled at each other at every opportunity.

Add to that Bill wrecking Elvis's beloved first car under a hay truck; the Florida fans annihilating his second car with lipstick and nail polish; and Sam Phillips contemplating selling Elvis's contract to some other label, so he could devote his time to Carl Perkins—June just had to be better.

A Jolly Holly Concert

June 3, 1955 - Lubbock - Johnson-Connelly Pontiac Showroom (7 p.m.)
June 3, 1955 - Lubbock - Fair Park Coliseum (8 p.m.)

Johnson-Connelly Pontiac Showroom in Lubbock

Elvis and the boys got a couple days off at the first of June, partially because they needed the rest and partially because their next performance was scheduled for Lubbock and it would take them that long to drive there.

The West Texas town made the most of the singers' appearance. They billed them as sort of a Grand Ole Opry/Louisiana Hayride extravaganza with Jim Ed and Maxine Brown, the Carlisles, and Ferlin "On the Wings of a Snow White Dove" Huskey. Bob Neal agreed to a free 7 p.m. show at the Johnson-Connelly Pontiac dealership before the 8 p.m. performance at the Fair Park auditorium. So the hundreds who arrived at the dealership got to sample an Elvis hors d'oeuvre before the main entree.

At the low end of the bill perched Scotty and Bill, but one group who didn't make the bill at all was Buddy and Bob, the warm-up band. Fifteen-year-old Buddy Holly, known to the Lubbock locals as "that little no-good punk who drives motorcycles up and down the street," divided his time between practicing in the garage with his ragamuffin band and avoiding arrest for disturbing the peace. Like Elvis, Buddy idolized James Dean, and for a while it looked like he'd follow the same path to the bitter end.

In a strange circle of fate, two years later Buddy Holly and a few of the future Crickets lay asleep in the back room of Norman Petty's recording studio in Clovis, New Mexico, hoping they'd get a break if they hung around long enough. In the next booth Sherry Davis, the Big D Jamboree warm-up singer for Elvis at the Cotton Bowl, prepared to record "Broken Promises" and "Humble Hearts" but found she had no backup musicians due to a scheduling snafu. They dragged the boys off the floor and invited them to

Recognize those specs? Buddy Holly wrestles through the crowd to get to E. Lubbock 1955
Courtesy of Jay Thompson

accompany her on the songs; Buddy Holly on lead, Jerry Allison on drums, George Atwood on bass, and Vi Petty on organ. Since the rules read that an artist couldn't sing on a label they weren't contracted for, their names never made it to the credits, until the oversight was discovered thirty years later. Buddy's untested voice rings clear in the background on the compilation CD "Gals of the Big D Jamboree," but the artist playing the guitar is still argued by music historians.

In still one more example of the past meeting the future, another musical voyeur to watch the show that day in Lubbock was Mac Davis. He caught the musical fire when Elvis performed at the Pontiac dealership. Later, Mac would tell DJ Larry Byers of radio station KDAV, "That's when I knew what I wanted to do with my life, play music." In the sixties Mac wrote multiple hit songs for Elvis, including "In the Ghetto," "Memories," and "Don't Cry Daddy."

Now, let's all break into a chorus of "It's a Small World."

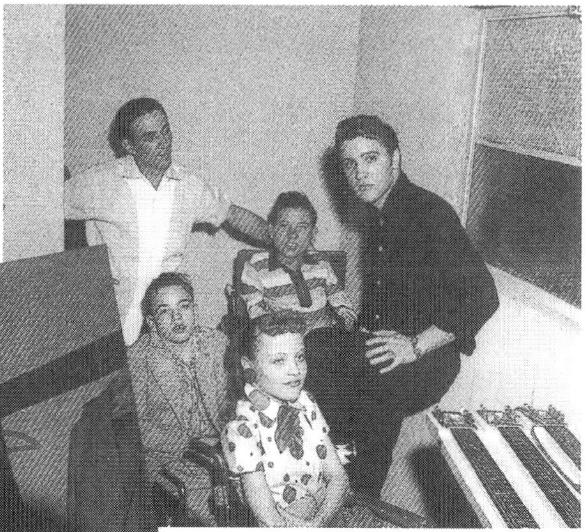

E. was a softee for good causes. Faron Young and E. playing host to a local crippled children's hospital field trip. Lubbock Coliseum.
Courtesy of I. G. Holmes

Photos cost one dollar, squeezes were free. Carolyn Pinkston (left), E., and Wanda Byers, wife of Lubbock DJ Larry Byers (right), Lubbock Coliseum. [illegible] I. G. Holmes

Smoke Gets in Your Eyes

June 16, 1955 - Texarkana - Municipal Auditorium

The crowd chanted, but Elvis was nowhere in sight. Jim LeFann of KOSY paced backstage, while Scotty and Bill tried not to look worried. They had arrived earlier, allowing Elvis some quality time with his beloved pink Cadillac. They knew that despite his penchant for speed, Elvis occasionally appeared late due to unforeseen haywagons on the roads between Louisiana and Texas. Tonight, though, he was positively missing.

Cheesie Nelson and his faithful sidekick, Pat Cupp, had entertained the audiences in the past with their impressions of Elvis and Scotty Moore, so Mr. LeFann sent the young men out onto the stage to warm the crowd up...but not too warm, mind you. As backup, he asked Scotty and Bill to play with Cheesie and stall for time until they could find out where their lead singer was hiding.

Miles away, Elvis sat on the side of the road, hugging his guitar and crying his eyes out. The last remnants of his beloved Cadi smoldered into a charred spot just a few feet away. Outside Hope, Arkansas, the Cadillac had caught on fire. When Elvis tried to lift the hood, the car went up like a torch. He had managed to save his guitar, but everything else perished in the blaze. Now he waved cars by until he got his composure back and then grudgingly thumbed a lift into Texarkana.

When his friends saw his face they knew something bad had happened. Elvis wore his Paul Bunyan-esque street clothes, instead of the flashy suit. His costume, like theirs, went up with the car.

In the spirit of the show must go on, the boys gathered themselves and gave the audience the show they came to see. If Elvis didn't really seem to exude the oomph that was his norm, certainly his sidekicks didn't blame him. They finished the show, signed the pictures, and shared his pain. Then his pals took him back to the hotel and tried to figure out how in the world they would be able to finish the back-to-back tour ahead of them.

Ironically, in one year's time Elvis would have the money to buy any car he could possibly desire, but he would lose something infinitely more valuable, his close friendship with Scotty and Bill.

Costumes, car, and confidence, all gone in a puff of smoke. Texarkana 1955. Courtesy of Marileon Hopkins Jerden

Famous Last Words

June 17 - Stamford - Roundup Hall

On June 17 Elvis and the Blue Moon Boys were scheduled to play their old stomping ground, the Stamford Roundup Hall, a Spartan affair without chairs or tables, where you could bring a bottle of booze, but you had to go to your car to drink it. Without transportation, the chance of arriving at the concerts booked for them through the 21st seemed impossible. So, after Thursday's Texarkana show, Scotty shipped back to Tennessee to borrow the pink and purple Crown Victoria Elvis bought his parents out of his share of the year's proceeds, about $200 a performance. Luckily Texas had no speed limits at that time, because Scotty must have averaged 100 mph. He drove all night from Memphis to Stamford, arriving barely in time to make the concert.

Possibly due to Scotty's exhaustion and Elvis's depression, the show that night elicited a polite but reserved response from the same crowd who had nearly climbed the walls three months before. The next morning the mayor from the town next door remarked to the breakfast crowd at the local café, "that boy will never make it." Six months later the teasing began, and it lasted for years. Hey Mayor Byre, did you see Presley on Ed Sullivan last night? I don't know, I just don't think he'll make it.

Elvis never appeared for the third booking in Stamford that autumn. When after years of playing high schools and car dealerships he suddenly became an "overnight success," Bob Neal, Elvis's manager, canceled the concert and paid the owner of the Roundup Hall for his trouble. At $500 a crack, the bigger gigs meant that Elvis could no longer afford to play the small towns.

Remember when...

no woman would be caught dead in public wearing pants? But girls on farms wore their brothers' hand-me-down bib overalls to work in the fields. To give them a custom fit, they hopped into a convienient body of water and shrunk them on their body.

Kilt Him a B'ar

June 20-21, 1955 - Beaumont - Municipal Auditorium

Sing along now....

Born on a mountaintop in Tennessee,
greatest state in the land of the free,
raised in the woods, so he knew every tree,
kilt him a b'ar, when he was only three.
Davy, Davy Crockett, King of the Wild Frontier.

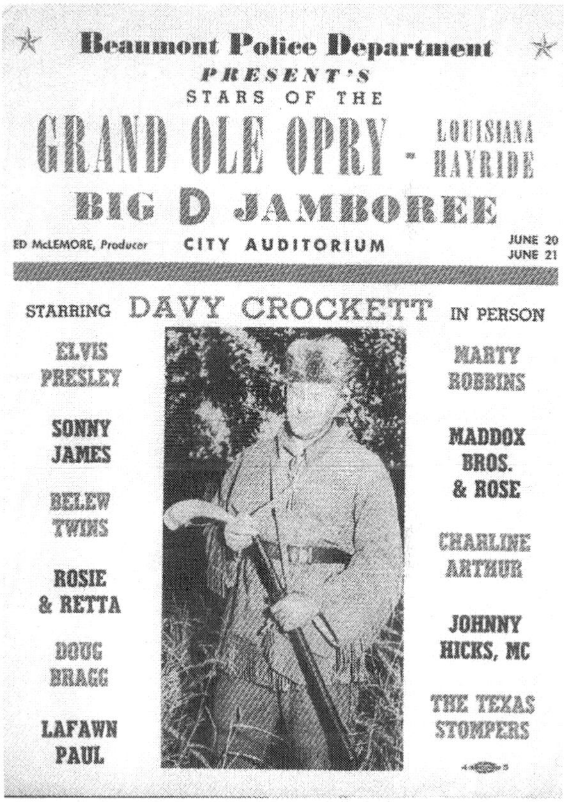

Cool buckskins. Ed Watt, promoter of the Big D Jamboree, Beaumont 1955.

Crockett-mania raged when Elvis and the Blue Moon Boys played the concerts in Beaumont. In a rare occurrence of the Big D Jamboree outside their usual Dallas stomping ground, the two-day benefit donated all proceeds to the Beaumont police department. As a gimmick, promoter Ed Watt donned his buckskins to grace the cover of the program.

Along with the Big D Jamboree gang, the "season's greatest hillbilly show" combined the considerable talents from the Louisiana Hayride and the Grand Ole Opry. They filled the hall to capacity for all five shows and made quite a considerable sum for the local constabulary. Guest singers included Elvis, Sonny James, Charlene Arthur, and complete unknown Marty Robbins.

Charlene had her own television show on Midland's Channel 2 by this time. A few months earlier in an attempt to expose Elvis to television, she dragged his very inexperienced self onto her show for an educational experience that neither he nor her audience would forget. Elvis appeared very young and very nervous in front of the camera. Who'd have thunk he was the same guy who starred in a movie a year later.

Beaumont Municipal Auditorium

In July 1955 -
The "Mickey Mouse Club" debuted on American television, and Disneyland in Anaheim, California, opened its doors.

How Sweet the Sound

July 4, 1955 - Stephenville - Rec Hall (morning)
July 4, 1955 - DeLeon - Hodge's Park (afternoon)

Stephenville Rec Hall

The Statesmen Quartet

Will appear in person
MONDAY, JULY 4th at HODGES PARK in De Leon and Stephenville Recreation Hall, Stephenville, Texas

Along with The Blackwood Brothers, The Deep South, Stamps and Stamps Ozark Quartets and R. W. Blackwood, Jr. Plus Elvis Presley, Slim Willet and The Farren Twins.

In case of rain, there will be one program only at the Stephenville Recreation Hall. Good weather prevailing this talent will alternate, each group appearing at Hodges Park and the Stephenville Recreation Hall. Both programs begin at 10 a. m. and run until 5 p.m. Admission will be 50c for children and $1 for adults at both places.

Take your choice, but be sure and attend one of these big programs.

Will the real Tennessee Ernie Ford please stand up? The five members of the Statesmen "Quartet."

For decades the "Battle of the Songs" raged in the Hodge family's pecan orchard. Tandem concerts played simultaneously in DeLeon, and Stephenville nursed toddlers like Slim Willet, the Statesmen, and Minnie Pearl into musical puberty until its demise in the sixties. The heralded favorite, a gospel group called the Blackwood Brothers, co-billed with the Statesmen for the July 4th 1955 concert. The two teams would start in Stephenville in the morning, then swap stages with the DeLeon group; the Stamps, Deep South Quartet, and the Farren Twins, in the parched afternoon. With Group A, a newcomer with long sideburns and a checkered shirt tagged along.

Hodge's Park Pecan Orchard.

The cool early morning burned away, and the orchard filled with sweaty music lovers fanning themselves against the scorching temperatures that only Texas in July can produce. To much ovation, the Statesmen ended their segment and the Blackwood Brothers, in dazzling white suits, slowly climbed onto the flatbeds that made up the stage. Each member selected his place, but instead of launching into ethereal harmony, a young man stepped to the front of the stage. Last year on the way to the concert in DeLeon, he told the audience, the Blackwood Brothers lost two of its own when their plane crashed in Alabama. One of the men killed was his father, R.W., a good and spiritual man taken before his work was finished on this earth. So in memory of his father and their departed brother, Bill Lyles, he would like to dedicate this song to two souls who once were lost, but now were found, were blind but now they see. When JD Sumner's profundo bass voice wrenched the chorus of "Amazing Grace" from the very core of the earth, tears flowed down every cheek. The crowd wept openly through heart-rending inspirational songs, whose words always hold new meaning when sung for those we've recently lost. Emptied, but somehow lightened, the brothers filed off the stage.

Next up, Elvis Presley was slated to leap on stage and bring down the house with the new rock-a-billy sound. He couldn't go through with it. Raised in the South where cars pulled to the side of the road in respect for funeral processions, Elvis told the promoter, J.W. Nowlin, that he thought his music hugely inappropriate for the moment, never mind that he had been friends with Cecil Blackwood since he was fifteen. When he was announced, Elvis stepped slowly to the microphone. Without preamble or trademark moves, he soothed into a program of wistful old-time-religion songs, the melodic notes sprinkling the upturned faces of his audience. The response from the 5,000 onlookers was the only cool air circulating on that 100+ degree day. Irony of ironies, Elvis sings the only all-gospel show of his life at a gospel show, and the audience hates him for it. The teenagers who came to hear him rock the orchard left in disappointment that he hadn't sung their favorites. The adults who came to hear the quartet ranged from unimpressed to insulted at hearing their lovely songs coming out of the mouth of a hoodlum. Who did he think he was, anyway, one of the Statesmen?

Elvis, Scotty, and Bill wasted little time departing for their third gig at the Soldiers and Sailors Auditorium in Brownwood that evening.

Brownwood Soldiers and Sailors Auditorium

We liked you better as a bad boy. DeLeon, July 1955

In August 1955 -
Chuck Berry released his first song, "Maybellene," to much acclaim. In the next several years he spun out a hit a year, including "Roll Over Beethoven" and "Johnny B. Goode."

The Truth is Out There

August 10, 1955 - Gladewater - Baseball Field

Powerful as he seemed, Tom Perryman could not control the weather or people's reaction to it. On a stifling hot August evening, the Gladewater DJ booked Elvis for another performance in his fair town. The previous performance in April proved such a barnburner that Perryman decided to lure the Hillbilly Cat to town whenever the schedule permitted.

Since many of the auditoriums still didn't have air conditioning, he organized the concert at the baseball park at night, when the 110-degree temperature would have dropped to a reasonable 95-100. At least a breeze (even one born in the Sahara) would keep the air moving.

The audience didn't quite see it that way. When Elvis took to the stage in the middle of the field, most of the town's folks lay prostrate across their hammocks at home. In that kind of heat, the only defense against heat stroke is to simply not move. After crawling home from work that Wednesday, stripping down to the legal limits, and having a light supper (with lots of ice cold cantaloupe and watermelon), the inhabitants of most of Texas lay inert in front of a fan.

Elvis's disappointment in the paltry turnout (twenty masochists) reflected in his quarter-hearted attempt at entertainment. He stood at the microphone and moaned a few bars, looking for signs of life in the pod people below. At half time he slunk off the stage, where Scotty took him aside and gave him a pep talk worthy of Vince Lombardi. Okay, so only five people

Gladewater Baseball Field

Real singer or alien replacement? E. signs a baseball. Gladewater 1955.
Courtesy of Steve Bonner

showed up and four of them arc deaf. The one who can hear paid good money to come here tonight and the other four can read pelvic sign language. So go out there, kid, and give 'em one for the Gipper (or something along those lines).

Scotty's little speech galvanized his friend. Elvis rocketed onto stage for the second half and ripped through his lineup with such enthusiasm, the audience wondered what he'd been smoking and how they could score some. The concept of an alien changeling was briefly entertained, but the show ended before anyone could tell if the creature in pink sported telltale ridges on the back of his neck. Dazed, the folks wandered home unsure of what they'd just experienced.

Gotcha'

August 11, 1955 - Longview - Reo Palm Isle

Where's my wife? The trucker shouted over the din to his friend's other half.

She looked around as if noticing her friend's absence for the first time. They'd all been oo-ing and ah-ing over the sexy young singer, named Elvis Presley, flirting with them throughout his songs. He'd give them that sizzling, sultry look from the stage, and they'd all giggle like teenagers. Their husbands just rolled their eyes.

Longview 1955. Courtesy of Karolee Flennigan

Maybe she got sick, she shouted back. I'll go check the powder room, she said pointing to the facilities.

He didn't hear her but nodded at her meaning. A few moments later she reappeared shaking her head.

Maybe she went to the car, she suggested when they got close enough to hear.

He nodded and wandered out to the parking lot, his friend following him for a breath of clean air and a smoke. As they approached

Jimmy Day and E. at the Reo Palm. Longview 1955 (despite the inscription added later)

the car, they noticed a stranger glancing out the window and then disappearing. The two increased their speed and ripped open the door. His wife screamed from the passenger side and dove for the petticoats in the floorboard. Elvis fell onto the dirt parking lot, struggling to zip up. The trucker reached down with huge, burly arms and grabbed the skinny frame, shaking the stuffing out of it and driving in a couple of well-placed right hooks.

Not my face, not my face, the singer yelled, covering the aforementioned location. I've gotta' go back and play.

The truck driver got in a few more gut-busters then let his quarry flee back to the club.

One thing you could say for Elvis, he certainly had a way of loosening the morals of the time. In subsequent years the beleaguered men of America would toast him for that attribute. But one man in Longview never would.

Jumpstarting His Career

August 22, 1955 - Wichita Falls - Spudder Baseball Field

Even though Mr. and Mrs. Presley had signed a contract with Colonel Parker just seven days before for their underage son, it was DJ Bill Mack who booked Elvis for the August 22 performance in Wichita Falls. Long before he became the "Midnight Cowboy" of WBAP or wrote "Blue" for Patsy Cline, Mack hosted the Big Six Jamboree, where he interviewed Elvis and invited the Hayride singer to play a set with Mack's band.

Mack called Tillman Franks, the mover and shaker of the Louisiana Hayride, and told him to send those boys and girls out to the Falls; they had a whole baseball stadium to fill up. One hot summer evening, Betty Amos, Johnny "the Singin' Fisherman" Horton, Elvis and the Blue Moon Boys, and Bill Mack and his band cranked the field lights at Spudder Park, the old Texas Baseball League field. Horace Logan, "that genial emcee" of the Hayride

Johnny "The Singin' Fisherman" Horton. Courtesy of Ms. Traci Nelson Dockery

Spudder Park, Wichita Falls, site of rampant "vulgarity."

climbed onto the flatbed that served as a makeshift stage and got the evening started. To the 2,000 folks, many of whom came to hear Johnny Horton, Elvis Presley was quite the eye-opener. He drove his pink Cadillac right up to the stage and leapt onto the flatbed. (Elvis had just bought the Cadi with his hard-earned money to replace the one that burned up in Arkansas. Now he would only part with it to perform important calls of nature . . . and then only with coaxing.)

For twenty minutes he raged, he rocked, he perpetually tugged on his pegged pants that kept trying to fall down around his ankles. The flatbed rocked so violently in response to his pelvic jerks that Mack's mother, who had come into town for the birth of his new daughter, repeated in disgust, vulgar, vulgar, vulgar. And did I mention, vulgar?

After the show, Mack asked Little Joe Carlson, one of the entertainers, if he wanted to go visit his new baby at the hospital. Elvis overheard and asked if he could tag along. They all piled into Mack's new Pontiac. After making a stop at the Beverly Drive-In for some chow, the threesome continued to the hospital, where they cooed like fools at the nursery window for several hours before returning to the park to pick up Elvis's car. But when they arrived, there sat the pink Cadi, its headlights barely glowing above lightning bug status and its battery shaking hands with its maker. Elvis had left the lights on.

Elvis asked Mack to give his car a push with the Pontiac, but Mack protested. No way. I'm not scratching my beautiful new car. Subsequently, the three men pushed the two-ton Cadi into the gravel road of the baseball park and stood around waiting for providence to fall in their lap. It showed up in the form of a farmer in an ancient truck, color virtually unrecognizable under the thirty plus years of North Texas dirt. The farmer obliged them by bumping the Cadillac down the road, and Elvis hopped in to turn the ignition over. Waving thanks, Elvis, Tillman Franks, and Mack decided that since they had to drive the car around to recharge the battery, they might as well go to the Toddle House for a late snack. At the restaurant the three stuffed their faces and Elvis cooed lovingly out the window at *his* baby.

At the end of '55, Colonel Parker called Mack and asked him if he would like Elvis to return to Wichita Falls. Mack agreed and offered to pay Elvis $600, to which Parker replied, "That's all right for me, but what about Elvis?"

Elvis did indeed return to Wichita Falls for the infamous January '56 show, when Hank Snow got booed off the stage.

Behind the Bleachers

August 26, 1955 - Gonzales - Baseball Field

Just up the road a piece from Nixon, Texas, Weldene Robinson and her friend opened the Gonzales newspaper and spotted an ad for a singer named Elvis Presley. They debated whether they wanted to spend that sweltering South Texas Friday night at the drive-in or watching some unknown performer play at the baseball park. The two girls opted for the drive-in, at least until they mentioned it to a new girl in school.

You don't know who Elvis Presley is? The recent immigrant from Corpus Christi exclaimed in shock and horror. Why, he's just . . . the *most.*

Since "the most" was about as good as you could get at that time, Weldene and her friend decided to give the concert a try. The drive-in wouldn't go anywhere while they were gone.

The show started after the broiling sun set and the temperature dropped to a breathable 95 degrees. Elvis drove his pink Cadillac right up to the flatbed truck stuck in the middle of the baseball field and leaped onto the springy stage. He jazzed the crowd for four or five numbers and then just as quickly, sprang back into his car and propelled it off the field.

From their vantage point in the bleachers the girls watched as the taillights disappeared behind the grandstand.

Let's go tell him how much we liked the show, the girls agreed and scampered down the backside of the bleachers toward the Cadillac. Chatting excitedly, they closed in on the car when they noticed someone else moving in on their target.

Who's that girl? They slowed their pace and watched the woman in skintight pedal pushers and peekaboo blouse sway toward the car. The door opened and the girl jumped in.

She must be from the next town over. No one in Gonzales would dress like that.

Curiosity spurred the ladies forward. They discovered that with the right combination of altitude, courtesy of the baseball bleachers,

Gonzales Baseball Field

Courtesy of Weldene Robinson

they could barely see inside the car window.

What are they doing? Weldene's friend asked, attempting to get a clear view.

Oh my goodness! Their question answered, the voyeurs backed away in shock.

Right there in public, and everything, she definitely is not from Gonzales.

And to think, I almost respected him.

The girls nodded sagely and decided to grab a bite at the drive-in after all.

In September 1955 -
The day after the filming for *Giant* finished, James Dean crashed his Porsche rocketing at 115 mph. He was killed instantly. The following month *Rebel Without a Cause* was released.

Near Miss

September 2, 1955 - Texarkana - Municipal Auditorium

In the same month that James Dean died in the wreckage of his smashed Porsche, Scotty, Bill, and Elvis ran into their own car problem... so to speak. Late for the Texarkana show, again, Scotty put the pedal to the metal of the Cadillac and blazed a trail through Arkansas. Traveling at speeds that certainly exceeded the minimum recommended daily allowance, Scotty didn't see the farm truck pull in front of them until they were already eating its tailpipe. The Cadillac slammed into the truck, throwing produce projectiles into the next county. Amazingly, no one was killed.

A year before seatbelts commonly adorned American models, many people lost their lives in collisions of this sort due to head trauma against the unpadded dashboard or decapitation from the "safety glass" in the windshield. The sheer weight and length of the Cadillac's iron frame kept Elvis from emulating his favorite icon and becoming a mere footnote of a footnote in the history books.

After a considerable period of time, a state trooper rolled past. He slowly pulled the cruiser off the road. The door swung open and he crawled out of his car, resettling his hat before easing across the tarmac to the accident. He walked around the prone car, shaking his head and sizing up the damage with little tsk-tsking noises and the occasional guttural "uh huh." The trooper didn't seem to be in too much of a hurry; not much happening in Fourke, Arkansas, that day, apparently. Elvis felt an urgency to get to the auditorium, though.

Look, can you please hurry this up. We have a gig in Texarkana that we're late for, Elvis told him. Southern bred as he was, Elvis should have known that this was precisely the wrong tone to take with a state trooper.

The cop stared at him, his blank expression scanning Elvis's sideburns, greasy hair, pink and orange plaid shirt....

Sit yourself down, the trooper told him. You can go when I let you, and I'll finish when I finish.

Hours later the Cadillac limped into Texarkana and passed out in back of the auditorium. The threesome grabbed their instruments and ran inside, where Jim LeFann of KOSY paced a pattern into the floorboards backstage. Once again, Cheesie Nelson entertained the throngs with his impression of Elvis, periodically glancing to the side stage in hopes that the cavalry would charge over the hill soon.

Elvis ran to the dressing room to change clothes, and Scotty and Bill assembled their set. Scotty thanked Cheesie for his help as the boy left the stage. Elvis came to the mike without his typical flamboyant entry and muttered into the microphone, "Well, it seems you folks have been well taken care of and I'd like to thank 'em." A little sincerity in his voice might have helped at this point, but the last couple of months had taken their toll on Elvis. He hadn't been eating well, and friends and family noticed that he'd grown terribly thin and drawn. Nevertheless, he played to please, as always. And once again, the Texarkana masses had nothing but good memories about the show that night.

Tomorrow night the Big D Jamboree in Dallas beckoned.

For tonight's show, only an arrest-me-red jacket would do. Texarkana 1955. Courtesy of Marileon Hopkins Jerden

All work and no eats makes a very thin Elvis. Texarkana, September 1955. Courtesy of Jane Hopkins

E. going for that starved supermodel look. Texarkana 1955. Courtesy of Marileon Hopkins Jerden

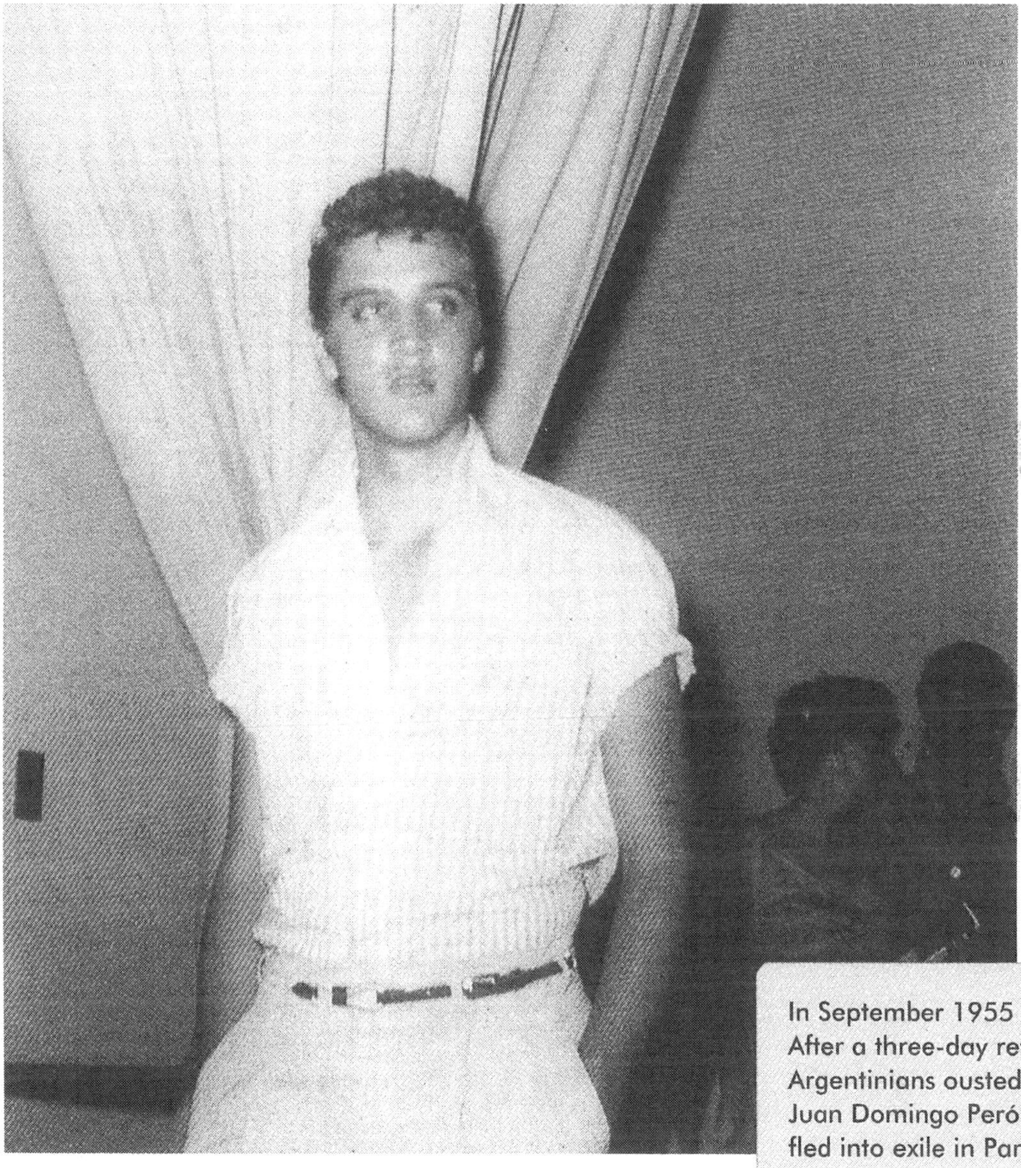

E. in his Tony Curtis perm period. Texarkana 1955.
Courtesy of Marileon Hopkins Jerden

In September 1955 -
After a three-day revolt, Argentinians ousted President Juan Domingo Perón, and he fled into exile in Paraguay. His wife, Eva (not Madonna), had died two years previously.

Bye Bye to Big D

September 3, 1955 - Dallas - Sportatorium

Big D Jamboree, Dallas 1955. Courtesy of Steve Bonner and David Denard

When Elvis played the September Big D Jamboree show, neither he nor they knew that it would be for the last time. Parker had taken over his contract in August, and since then he'd single-mindedly pursued larger and more profitable venues for his boy. But the calendar already stood full, committing Elvis through the autumn at smaller sites.

Bob Neal had already renegotiated Elvis's Louisiana Hayride contract, so that when it expired in November, the Hillbilly Cat would receive $200 a performance (as opposed to the original $18) in order to support drummer D. J. Fontana as a standard fixture in the group. Scotty and Bill's contract became fixed, and the summer of discontent rapidly slid into the icy waters of winter.

Meanwhile, Parker worked on Sam Phillips to sell Elvis's Sun contract to a big label like RCA. But negotiations dragged on.

Elvis, Scotty, and Bill returned to Dallas to play the September 3 Big D Jamboree show, but unbeknownst to them, Parker had already called Ed Watt, the show's promoter, attempting to renegotiate the late autumn show agreement for which Elvis was already scheduled. When Ed Watt asked how much Parker wanted for the next appearance, Parker quoted him $600. Ed told the Colonel "go to hell and take Elvis with you."

That night when Elvis packed away his amp and guitar, waved goodbye to his cohorts, and hopped over to the Roundup Club on Ervay Street, he actually waved goodbye to the life as he had known it.

E. and Bill at the Big D Jamboree, Dallas 1955. Courtesy of Steve Bonner and David Denard

In October 1955 -
After losing the World Series of 1916, 1920, 1941, 1947, 1949, 1952, and 1953, the Brooklyn Dodgers finally beat their old nemesis, the New York Yankees, in the only World Series they would ever win. In the seventh game of the series, Sandy Amoros in left field caught Yogi Berra's long fly, Gil Hodges drove in both runs, and Johnny Podres pitched a shutout. The illustrious lineup also included Hall of Famers: Jackie Robinson, who broke the color barrier in Major League Baseball, Roy Campenella, Carl Furillo, Pee Wee Reese, Sandy Koufax, Don Newcombe, and Duke Snider.

The next year Yankee pitcher Don Larsen pitched the first perfect no-hit, no-run game in Series history, ensuring that not one Dodger would get to first base. In 1958 the Dodgers moved to Los Angeles.

The Last Time I Saw Paris

October 4, 1955 - Paris - Boys Club Gym Auditorium

Paris Boys Club Auditorium

To help offset the debt incurred by building the Boys Club Auditorium, the club sponsored a benefit fund raiser. They had booked Elvis months before, so by the concert date, the auditorium swelled until bursting with fans dying to see the Hayride headliner.

The bleachers long since packed with teeming teenagers, chairs filled every nook and cranny of the hall. People lined the wall, willing to stand through as many hours as Elvis was willing to play.

Elvis knocked their proverbial socks off. With a list of recent recordings, including "Mystery Train," "I Forgot to Remember to Forget," and "When It Rains It Really Pours" to add to his repertoire, Elvis could give them an oldies and newies show that made everyone happy.

During the show he sweated buckets in the un-air-conditioned October swelter (remember, men didn't wear deodorant at this time; they thought it was too sissified). When girls grabbed for him, he literally slipped from their grasp. After the show he moved the autograph session out to his car, where he flipped his collar up over the aggravated acne and restlessly signed photo after photo (which still only cost a dollar). Some of the women asked Elvis for a ride in his snazzy pink Cadi, and he obligingly drove them around the block. But when he returned, he paced back and forth until the crowd cleared. Elvis and Bill jumped in the car and sped off into the night to Moseleys, a beer joint on the other side of the Red River. Ironically enough, Elvis liked to visit these places even though he didn't drink. (But then again, he handed cigarettes out and didn't smoke either.)

Paris Boys Club Auditorium

Jailhouse Rock

October 5, 1955 - Greenville - Municipal Auditorium

While the screaming teenagers at Greenville stood squashed together inside the auditorium, several gentlemen of leisure enjoyed Elvis's concert from their box seats under the building. Constructed at a time when all your municipal needs could be fulfilled in the same building, the auditorium sat on top of the city jail cells. To get to the stage, Elvis had to march through the prison and up a staircase leading to the hall, where the sound clearly reverberated to the basement. And they didn't have to pay the dollar cover charge either.

After the October show, one inmate showed his appreciation for the excellent entertainment by carving Elvis's name into the jail wall, where it remains to this day.

Cellblock C gives "a big thumbs up for that Presley boy." Greenville city jail.

Trouble in Paradise

October 6, 1955 - San Marcos - Southwest Texas State University
October 6, 1955 - Austin - Skyline Club

By autumn the music tour bit began to wear thin on Elvis, Scotty, and Bill. When Parker became Elvis's manager in August, he reserved the right to book the boys in any of forty-seven cities without telling them ahead of time where they were going to play next. As a result, Elvis and his sidekicks crisscrossed the South in a hectic schedule that set them at each other's throats. People who knew Elvis began to comment on how thin and drawn he looked. He didn't sleep well, and despite his penchant for fried southern foods, he dropped pounds off with a speed that a Weight Watchers enrollee would envy.

To make matters worse, Parker reformatted their standard show setup, pushing Scotty and Bill slowly to the back. Gone was the corny humor warm-up that relaxed the hyperactive Presley. The advertisements now read "The Elvis Presley Show" with the Blue Moon Boys scribbled in two-point type size at the bottom. The promotional pictures now showed only Elvis. Scotty and Bill sat on a fixed salary and watched Elvis become a millionaire before their eyes. People recognized Elvis's name, but the Blue Moon Boys sunk into obscurity. After working so hard to catch the public's eye, the quiet southern boy already chafed at the nonstop attention. He mentioned to friends and fellow musicians that the spotlight was getting old.

Although the afternoon San Marcos concert in the Southwest Texas State University auditorium went off without a hitch, the threesome squabbled before, during, and afterwards. Elvis,

San Marcos Auditorium at SW Texas State University

Oh, I tried to send my mom a rose.... Skyline Club, Austin, October 1955

But the boys and I came near to blows.... Skyline Club, Austin, October 1955

Scotty, and Bill arrived at the concert together, but after the show, when they were supposed to drive up to Austin for a gig at the Skyline Club that evening, Elvis spotted a flower street vendor. On a whim, he decided to fill the car with flowers for his mother, leaving Scotty and Bill to hitch a ride with the other musicians. The Blue Moon Boys had words with their lead singer at the Austin venue.

Tillman Franks, promoter of the Louisiana Hayride tour decided to give the boys a "time-out" to cool down. Once the last chords of the Austin concert absorbed into the club walls, Tillman convinced Elvis to join him on a bus trip to Houston, where he was scheduled to play the day after next. Elvis consented, and they caught an eastbound Greyhound. A member of the troop drove the carload of flowers back to Memphis.

Elvis leaned his head against a window and took a catnap. Occupying most of the seats in the bus sat a girls' high school volleyball team. Tillman couldn't resist the temptation. An hour into the ride, he leaned over to the girl sitting primly across from him.

You know, he whispered conspiratorially, Elvis is on the bus.

The girl gave him a fish-eyed stare and loudly popped a pink gum bubble in response. Yeah, sure. And my mother is the senator from New York.

Really, that's him sleeping right there. Tillman insisted.

The girl next to her overheard and remarked, If that's him, make him sing something.

Tillman shook Elvis awake and told him to belt out a bar or two. Grudgingly, he opened his mouth and a few notes spilled out. The entire bus, to a woman, screamed. They flung their bodies over the dividing seats and begged for photographs and a song, or two, or three. Elvis sang an impromptu a capella program and threw dirty looks at the laughing Tillman the rest of the trip to Houston.

The breather seemed to help. By the time Elvis, Scotty, and Bill reassembled for the concert in Houston, they were ready to shake and make nice again, just in time for a grueling ten-concert trek across the state.

Skyline Club - Austin, October 1955

Dancehall Daze

October 9, 1955 - Cherry Springs - Cherry Springs Dance Hall

The Louisiana Hayride left the Houston show and caravanned to Cherry Springs, a little town stashed in the Hill Country between Fredericksburg and Mason. Just as in Paris, the dance hall booked to house the concert couldn't contain the masses that appeared. Kids hung in windows and stood outside to hear the show, screaming and shaking the historical rafters. The girls grew frenzied at such a speed that their boyfriends became alarmed . . . and jealous. One delightful child carved his initials into Elvis's shiny pink Cadillac with his pocketknife to make sure the musician knew how he felt about his girlfriend's abandonment. Elvis discovered the little present when he moved outside to sign autographs.

The show that night boasted Jimmy and Johnny, whose absence from the Hayride gave Elvis his first big break, Johnny Horton and Betty Amos, Horace Logan as emcee, and Billy Birdbrain (a.k.a. Tillman Franks). Many performers doubled as both a musician and a comedian and used a pseudonym as cover. Another name to spot in the Hayride advertisements was Simon Crum, otherwise known as Ferlin Huskey.

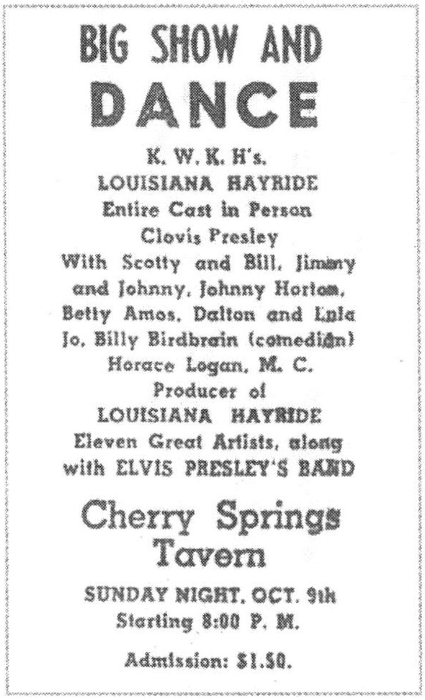

BIG SHOW AND
DANCE
K. W. K. H's.
LOUISIANA HAYRIDE
Entire Cast in Person
Clovis Presley
With Scotty and Bill, Jimmy and Johnny, Johnny Horton, Betty Amos, Dalton and Lula Jo, Billy Birdbrain (comedian) Horace Logan, M. C. Producer of LOUISIANA HAYRIDE Eleven Great Artists, along with ELVIS PRESLEY'S BAND
Cherry Springs Tavern
SUNDAY NIGHT, OCT. 9th
Starting 8:00 P. M.
Admission: $1.50.

Wow, Clovis Presley in person!

Cherry Springs Dance Hall

Oct 8 - Houston (After the concert, drive 266 miles on Highway 290, or approximately 5½-6 hours to the Hill Country. Remember, there were no interstate highways yet.)

Oct 9 - Cherry Springs (Then, drive 95 miles on Highway 377 toward West Texas.)

Oct 10 - Brownwood (Then, a short 2-hour drive up Highway 279 and 36 to Abilene.)

Oct 11 - Abilene (3½ hours to Midland.)

Oct 12 - Midland (5½ hours up to the Panhandle on Highway 349 and 87.)

Oct 13 - Amarillo (Retrace your path 258 miles back past Midland.)

Oct 14 - Odessa (Turn around and drive 136 miles, halfway back to Amarillo. But, hey, Buddy Holly is worth it.)

Oct 15 - Lubbock (afternoon concert)

Oct 15 - Lubbock (After the evening concert, it's time to drive that 8++ hours to our northern neighbor.)

Oct 16 - Oklahoma City

Who booked this schedule, Exxon?

The rest of the Hayride performers headed out to Nacogdoches for another show, but Elvis had already committed to a gig in Brownwood with friend Sid Foster of Breckenridge. He and Sid spent the day window shopping at Cadillac dealerships and discussing Parker's plan to move Elvis to a larger label.

Poor "Borter Wagoner." No one ever spells his name correctly.

Be My Little Good Luck Charm

October 11, 1955 - Abilene - Fair Park Auditorium

Back in June, Elsie Medlin and her friend Jane Giles were hanging out at the local radio station in Stamford, pestering the DJ to play their favorite songs. A couple years before the Top 40 concept swallowed the airways, DJs played anything they pleased, and if a pretty girl asked for something special, they often got their wish.

Three gentlemen walked into the studio who made the girls sit up and take notice. One of them wore a purple suit with red socks and greasy hair. Elsie thought he "looked just like an alligator." The strangers cut a promo spot for their performance at the Stamford Roundup Hall that night, and the two eavesdroppers became intrigued. They ran home and begged their parents to let them go to the show. Their parents consented, but only because the Roundup didn't allow alcohol, and only if Judy's older brother went with them as chaperone. Grudgingly they accepted the conditions, and despite the tame response by the evening's crowd, Elsie and Jane became hooked. They boldly introduced themselves to Elvis, Scotty, and Bill after the show and wheedled out of them that they were staying at the Stale Motel. (Doesn't that sound like a place you want to lay your head?)

The next morning the girls kidnapped their friend Valerie Harms into driving them around and around the block in her turquoise T-bird, waiting for the elusive singer to appear from his motel. Valerie and her friend had spontaneously started a fan club the night Elvis performed in Stamford the previous April. She now drove in mad circles, armed with club cards she had induced the local newspaper to create for her.

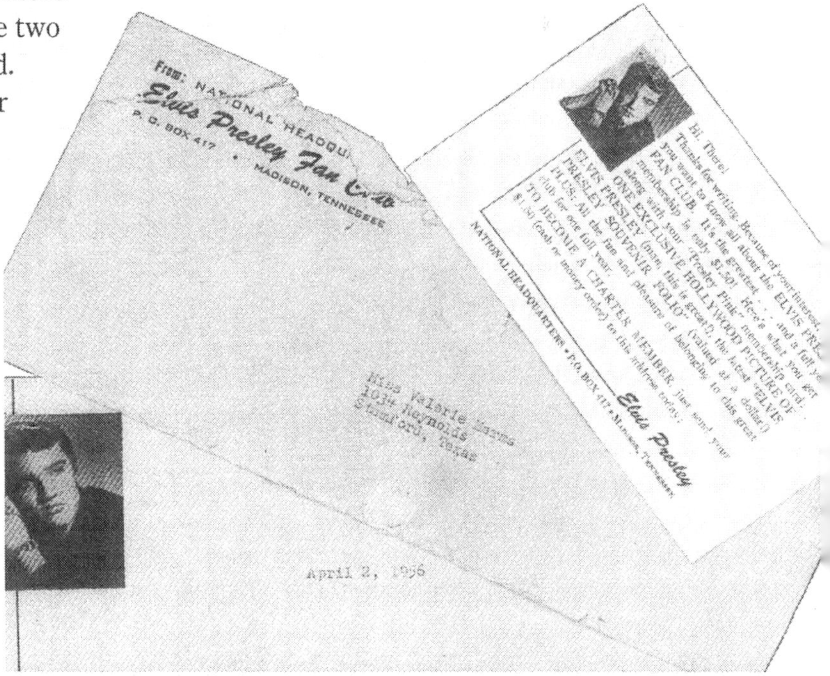

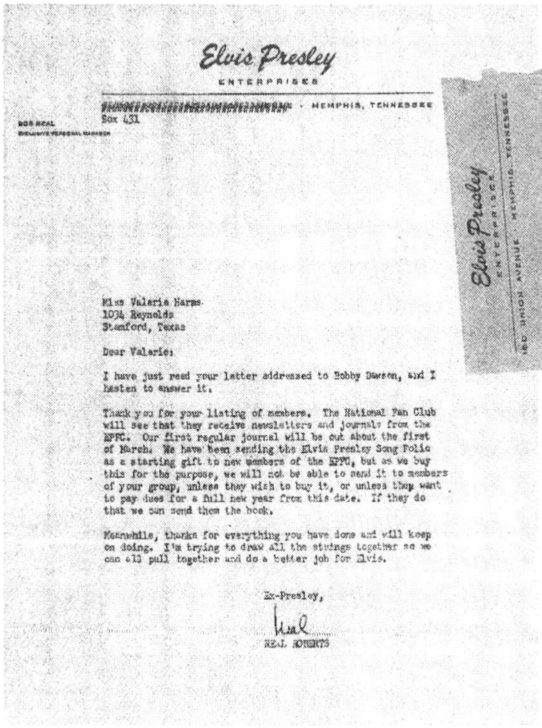

Elvis Presley
ENTERPRISES
[redacted] · MEMPHIS, TENNESSEE
BOB NEAL
Box 431

Miss Valeria Harms
1034 Reynolds
Stanford, Texas

Dear Valerie:

I have just read your letter addressed to Bobby Dawson, and I hasten to answer it.

Thank you for your listing of members. The National Fan Club will see that they receive newsletters and journals from the EPFC. Our first regular journal will be out about the first of March. We have been sending the Elvis Presley Song Folio as a starting gift to new members of the EPFC, but as we buy this for the purpose, we will not be able to send it to members of your group, unless they wish to buy it, or unless they want to pay dues for a full new year from this date. If they do that we can send them the book.

Meanwhile, thanks for everything you have done and will keep on doing. I'm trying to draw all the strings together so we can all pull together and do a better job for Elvis.

Ex-Presley,

Neal

NEAL ROBERTS

Early Fan Club letter on pink stationery. Notice that Bob Neal was still listed as manager and it was mailed from Memphis. Courtesy of Elsie Medlin

Even the envelopes were pink.

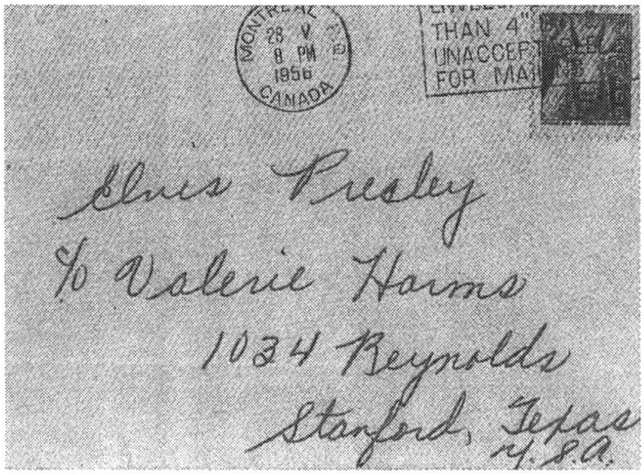

I'm sure Valerie wouldn't mind being "in care of" Elvis Presley.

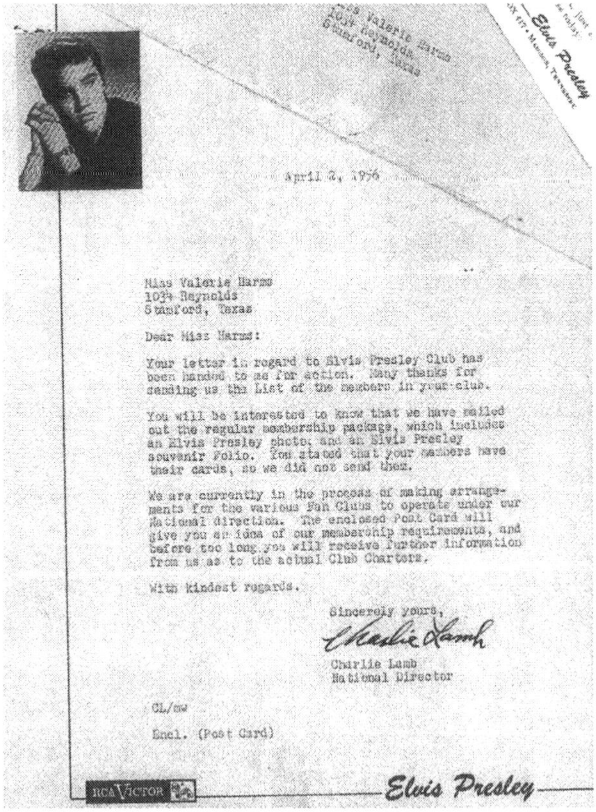

April 2, 1956

Miss Valerie Harms
1034 Reynolds
Stamford, Texas

Dear Miss Harms:

Your letter in regard to Elvis Presley Club has been handed to me for action. Many thanks for sending us the List of the members in your club.

You will be interested to know that we have mailed out the regular membership package, which includes an Elvis Presley photo, and an Elvis Presley souvenir Folio. You stated that your members have their cards, so we did not send them.

We are currently in the process of making arrangements for the various Fan Clubs to operate under our National direction. The enclosed Post Card will give you an idea of our membership requirements, and before too long you will receive further information from us as to the actual Club Charters.

With kindest regards.

Sincerely yours,

Charlie Lamb

Charlie Lamb
National Director

CL/mw

Encl. (Post Card)

RCA VICTOR — Elvis Presley

Later fan club letters issued by Parker out of Madison looked a bit more polished (but were still pink).

About 1,000 revolutions and two inches of worn pavement later, Elvis appeared, following his nose to the Stamford Coffee shop, where anyone who is anyone goes for breakfast. The three predators crept down the street, stalking their prey, and pulled silently into a parking spot behind the coffee shop. Flying casually, they sauntered into the restaurant and surreptitiously claimed a table behind the singer. Engrossed in his eggs and grits, he never noticed the girls, camouflaged as diners, slowly scooting their chairs and table closer to his, until Elsie's chair banged into his. Oh excuse me, sir, I didn't see you there.

Amused by the obvious tactics (the girls' table had somehow migrated ten feet across the floor), Elvis teased and joked with them through breakfast, the conversation rapidly declining into silly comments that teenage boys use to impress their female counterparts. Elvis threw salt over his shoulder, "for luck" he said. Then he added sagely, "You know, if you throw salt on a birds' tail, you could catch it."

When Valerie confessed to inventing fan club cards, he asked to see them. She produced a teetering stack. With good-natured humor, he whipped out a pen and signed every one.

Eventually they all parted company. Elvis had a show that evening in Dallas at the Sportatorium, and they had fan club cards to distribute.

On October 11, 1955, Valerie drove Elsie and Jane to the Fair Park Auditorium in Abilene, where Elvis was scheduled to play with a motley lineup including, Jimmy "A Fallen Star" Newman, Porter "Eat, Drink and Be Merry" Waggoner, Wanda Jackson, and Bobby Lord. Floyd Cramer and Jimmy Day temporarily ditched the Hayride to play piano and steel guitar respectively. Also appearing that evening was the virtual unknown Johnny Cash, a rough cob of a man with a talent for a catchy melody and memorable lyrics.

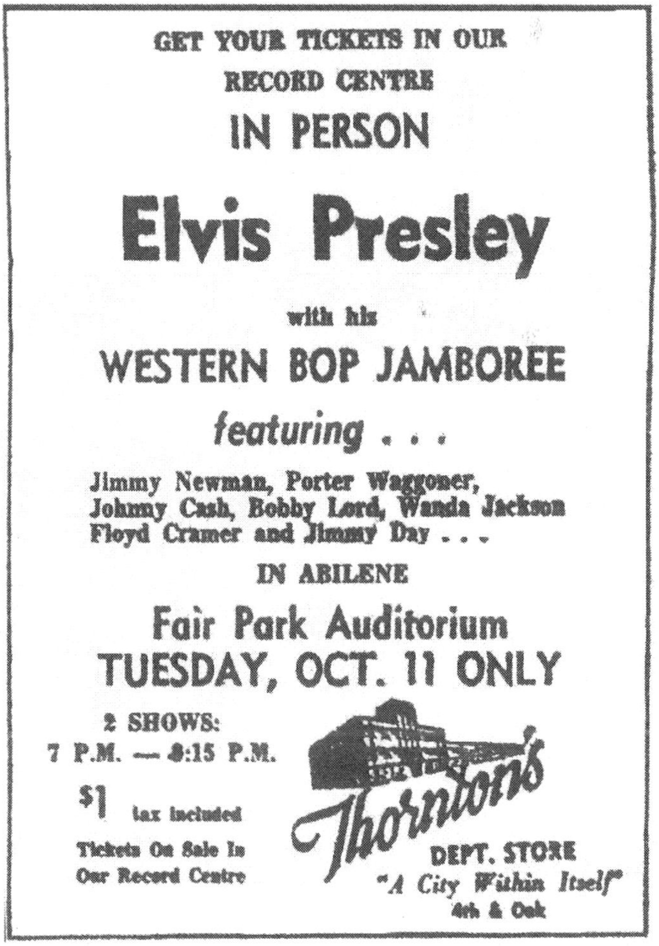

Wanda Jackson attends to her fans.

The girls arrived as a bevy of ponytails jockeyed to the stage door. Elvis pointed to his favorite fems and announced "Let these three backstage." The dauntless dames needed no second invitation. They scooted to the back, where Elvis lined them up and kissed them in succession, Elsie's very first kiss. He borrowed Elsie's lipstick and autographed a picture for her, in Passion Pink. When Johnny Cash walked by, Elvis pulled them close and whispered to them to stay away from that man, because he was on drugs. Wide-eyed, they obeyed.

The show that night landed Abilene on the map. As soon as Elvis showed his face on stage, the crowd went spastic. They chanted, they danced, they screamed, and that was just the opening number. Two songs into the set, the audience slipped out of control. During a rowdy rendition of "I've Got a Woman," Elvis ripped off his bow tie and threw it into the crowd. When they began to climb the stage to help him undress faster, he lobbed a shoe into the audience in self-preservation. It bounced off an old lady's head and propelled her backwards. Horrified at his aim, Elvis stopped the show to determine how badly she'd been hurt.

Floyd Kramer at the Hayride, 1955. Courtesy of Pat Green

A private serenade for his favorite fans. Faron Young (left), Jane Giles, Elsie Medlin, Valerie Harms, and E. backstage at Fair Park Coliseum, Lubbock 1956. Courtesy of I. G. Holmes

The ornery octogenarian sat up immediately, declared herself perfectly healthy, thank you very much, but nothing could persuade her to part with the shoe. Elvis continued the set in one stocking foot, but ceased the clothing projectiles before the crowd could demand more personal garments.

The teeny-bops grew bold at the Abilene show. They unbuttoned their blouses and enticed Elvis to sign their bras and their breasts. For days they'd wear peekaboo blouses to show off the autograph. Some taped paper or gauze over the signature so it wouldn't wash off.

Watch that hand, young lady! Jane Giles (left), Elsie Medlin, and Valerie Harms getting up close and personal. Lubbock 1956. Courtesy of I. G. Holmes

Elsie, Scotty, and D. J. Fontana take a 'cig' break. Wichita Falls, January 1956. Courtesy of Elsie Medlin

Elsie and Jane visited Elvis at his Lubbock performance and then again at the fateful January 19 Hank Snow Jamboree in Wichita Falls. Despite the ice that covered most of the state, Elsie begged her dad, a notorious softee, to let her and Jane go see Elvis. Worried that his stubborn daughter would get into an accident, Elsie's father volunteered one of his employees to drive the two girls the 100+ miles to the auditorium. When they arrived the concert had already begun. As Hank Snow opened, Scotty and Bill spotted the girls and ushered them backstage. They told Elsie and Jane that Elvis was very late and Hank Snow was furious. Elsie exclaimed that the road was a virtual ice rink. "It's a miracle that we even got to the show." Elvis eventually arrived safely, although he was over an hour late.

By the autumn of '56, Elvis had become famous nationwide. When Jane and Elsie drove to Dallas to see Elvis at the Cotton Bowl, they had to arrange a backstage pass with the National Fan Club. Since they had started one of the original chapters, the officials permitted the Stamford Fan Club delegates to watch the show from behind the curtain. With gaggles of guards and thousands of fans, the performances lost the intimacy of the high school auditorium. Elvis no longer hung around to mingle in the crowd. As soon as his set ended, he disappeared.

Elsie and Jane asked Scotty and Bill where they were staying and Scotty answered, We can't tell you girls. But, Bill and I are staying at the Stoneleigh Hotel, he added with a wink.

The girls arrived at the lobby and tried to act nonchalant. They didn't know what room

Jane (behind Elvis on right) and Elsie (far right) on serious fan club business. Lubbock 1956. Courtesy of I. G. Holmes

they had given up on plan A (due to serious lack of funds) and were moving to plan B, a man in the lobby started a conversation with them. He told them he was Nick Adams, a famous actor, and asked would they be interested in meeting Elvis Presley? Playing dumb, they nodded. Nick took them upstairs. When Elvis opened the door and saw the girls, he broke into a wide grin, "I can't believe you came all the way from Stamford to see me."

Nick's jaw dropped. He stared at the man and asked, "Hell, Elvis, do you know every girl in Texas?"

Elvis invited them into the room, where they sprawled in overstuffed chairs and discussed how much things had changed. D. J. Fontana and Hank Thompson arrived, and it turned into a little nostalgia party. As the evening wore on, Nick wondered aloud where Colonel Parker had stashed himself. Elvis retorted, "He's probably downstairs counting money." Someone snorted,

Elvis had escaped to, so they ran through some strategies. A. Bribe the hotel clerk. B. Knock on every door in the hotel until they find him. C. Hide in a room service cart and call in a late night order for Mr. Presley. But, just when

prompting gales of giggles from the rest of the party.

When Elsie and Jane weren't visiting the shows or pestering Scotty, they sent little pep-talk letters to their favorite singer to keep

The Stoneleigh Hotel in Dallas

up his spirits. When he appeared on the Dorsey Show in New York on February 18, 1956, they sent him a heartfelt telegram that read:

> **Hurry Home. Stop. Leave those damn Yankees alone. Stop.**
> **We Love You.**

The last time Elsie and Jane spoke with Elvis, he had just been drafted. They tracked down the house he had rented for his parents in Kileen, near the base. Discovering that he wasn't home, they turned to leave in disappointment. At that moment, Elvis drove up in a red Lincoln convertible. He invited them into the house, where they sat and visited for a while. Elvis spoke about the army and told them the Colonel advised him not to join the special services, so he wouldn't give all his talent away.

Elvis's mother hollered that supper was ready and he told them, "I'd better go. I don't want to keep Mama waiting. She hasn't felt well." Three weeks later his mother passed away. The girls never saw Elvis again.

KSIJ, Radio Sanctuary

November 19, 1955 - Gladewater - High School Gymnasium

Gladewater had sponsored the Louisiana Hayride show once before with huge success. So when the Hayride promoters announced a repeat performance at the Gladewater gymnasium in November '55, a circus atmosphere filled the air. No longer just an "East Texas discovery," Elvis's records now sold all over the country. He was becoming big, and his impending stardom could be tangibly felt through the pores. Everyone but everyone planned on invading Gladewater for the concert.

Elvis had just completed a successful concert in Cleveland with Bill Haley and Pat Boone. *Billboard* had just ranked him as the #1 Most Promising Country and Western Artist. And after months of finagling, Parker and RCA finally agreed on a new three-year recording contract for their boy. Elvis would receive a 5 percent royalty and extra pocket change for every Hill and Range composition he

LIVE BROADCAST

Hayride Show Here Saturday

All the big stars of KWKH's Louisiana Hayride show will be here in person Saturday night, when the entire show is broadcast from the stage of the local high school auditorium.

Elvis Presley and the entire Saturday night cast are slated to appear. This is the second live broadcast of the Hayride, popular hillbilly radio show, from Gladewater. Both shows have been sponsored by the Gladewater Junior Chamber of Commerce.

Tickets are now on sale for the show, and a large crowd is expected. At the first performance here, an overflow crowd, with people coming from all over the southwest, jammed the local gym, and the JC's cleared over $1,500 on proceeds of the show. This money has been spent for numerous civic projects in Gladewater, including assistance in the Little League baseball program, and other things for the betterment of the community.

Proceeds from tomorrow night's show will be used for similar projects.

Special souvenir programs are being printed for the show and will be sold at the show. A feature of the program is a large picture of Elvis Presley, a big drawing card with the Hayride show.

The public is invited to attend the show.

- **November 18, 1955, Gladewater Daily Mirror**

recorded. Leiber and Stoller furiously scribbled songs exclusively for Elvis to record, and "Heartbreak Hotel" lay in Elvis's hot little hand, waiting for his first RCA recording session. Tomorrow, he'd cross the t's and dot the i's on the paperwork with RCA, then his entire Sun label portfolio would be hauled over to RCA (where it lay rotting and forgotten in a storeroom until completely unrecognizable).

The more the excitement, the more Elvis looked for an escape. He sought refuge at his favorite haunt, radio station KSIJ in Gladewater, where Tom Perryman made sure the jackals remained at bay.

Free from pressures of fans or new manager, Elvis practiced in the mahogany-lined walls of the KSIJ sound studio and wandered the halls, sipping Coke from frosty green bottles and slapping his hands on his legs to an internal song. Sometimes he hid in the inner offices.

Elvis told secretary Shirley Graham, "Don't let anyone know I'm here; I'm tired."

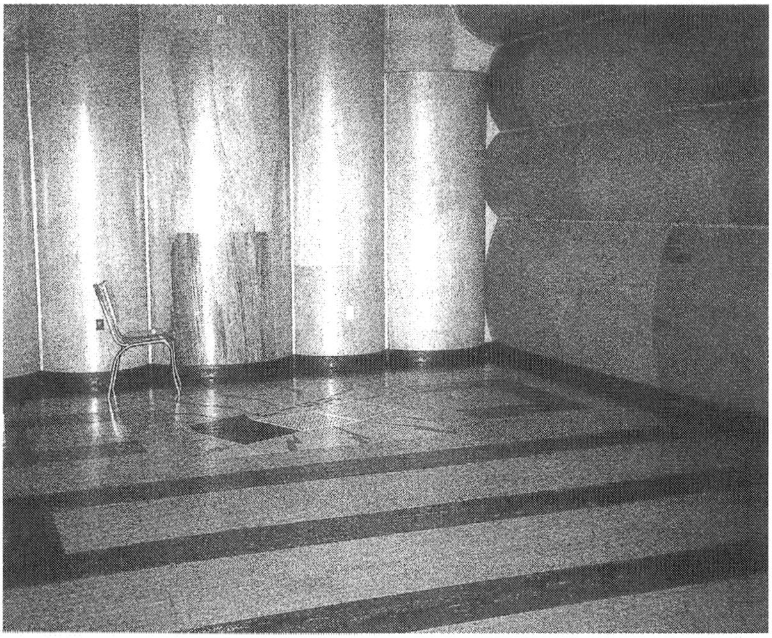

Elvis's favorite hiding spot in the hallowed halls of KSIJ radio

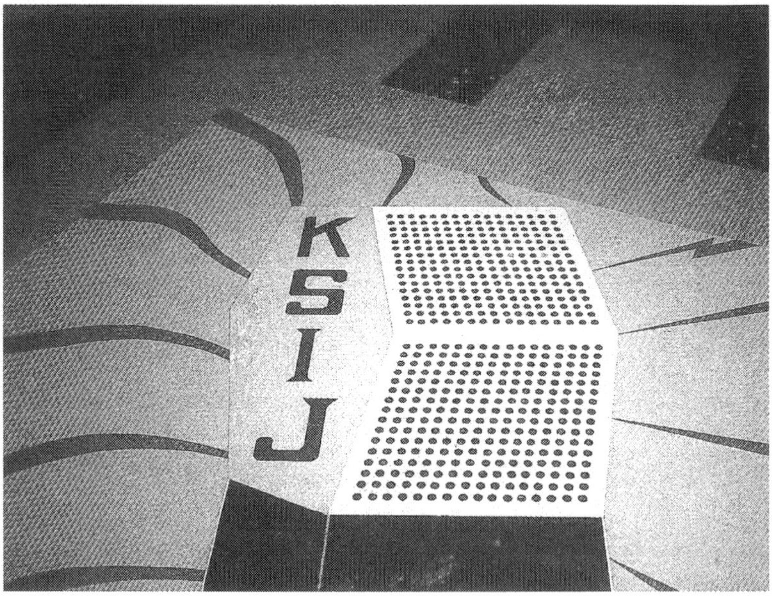

A tiled mosaic floor welcomed you to KSIJ radio in Gladewater.

Meanwhile, he stretched out on the floor and read comic books. When the phone rang as it inevitably did, Shirley told the inquirer, "He's not here. He went that-a-way," pointing down the hall for the listener to see. Elvis rolled on the floor behind her and laughed silently until she hung up.

The following year Shirley protected more than his privacy. During one of the last few Hayride shows in which Elvis appeared, Tom Perryman asked if Shirley would stay in Elvis's dressing room while he performed to prevent the rampant removal of his clothing by rabid teens looking for souvenirs. Shirley was scandalized. Waiting around in a man's dressing room just wasn't done by respectable women. Eventually her employer won the argument (mainly because he signed the paychecks). She baby-sat Elvis's droopy drawers until he returned.

The night of the Gladewater show, excited teens filed into the gymnasium as tubs of beer were rolled backstage to keep the singers' palates wet. Two tubs later and fifteen minutes into the sold-out show, those palates were positively soaked in hops. Performers swayed backstage, straightening up only when the emcee queued them. Even Horace Logan, "that genial emcee" got toasted, although he covered it much better than others.

Since Elvis didn't drink, he spent his time pacing. When Horace announced him, the resounding roar chipped the plaster and sent the roof across the border into Louisiana. Elvis gracefully moved to the stage, built in the center of the expansive floor, and promptly tripped on the stairs, sprawling into an ungainly heap in front of 3,000 expectant faces. A sympathetic wave of "ooooo" swept the audience, except for one parental voice that loudly remarked, "The devil's child is drunk and can't stand on his own two feet!"

The rest of the concert continued without incident or Dick Van Dyke impression.

In December 1955 -
Rosa Parks refuses to relinquish her seat to a white passenger in Alabama. A boycott begins that nearly bankrupts the Montgomery city bus lines.

Three to get ready . . .

Courtesy of Jimmy Willis and James F. Jasek

RCA Presents

Two days after his twenty-first birthday, Elvis entered the shabby and stilted recording studio of RCA to do his first set. A far cry from the carefree and playful Sun studios under Sam Phillips' guidance, the RCA people got bent out of shape when Elvis wouldn't stand in one place while he sang. After a series of inaudible takes, they remiked the room so that he could dance while he recorded.

Scotty Moore, Bill Black, D. J. Fontana, Floyd Cramer, and Gordon Stoker from the Jordanaires all felt the pressure as backup ensemble to get the prerequisite songs under their belt. They recorded "I've Got a Woman" to warm themselves up and rolled into "Heartbreak Hotel," a strange change of pace from his usual style. They completed "Money Honey" at the end of a very long first day and squeezed in "I Was the One" and "I'm Counting on You" on the following.

Mentally and physically exhausted, Scotty, Bill, and Elvis embarked on a fateful week-long tour with Hank Snow, the last time Elvis would ever play with the man, or play second fiddle in another man's concert.

In January 1956 -
The Olympics in Cortina, Italy got off to a shaky start when, despite the blizzards that had been attacking Europe, Italian soldiers had to truck snow in from the Alps to cover the dry ground of the Winter Games. When it quickly melted on the downhill course, a French skiing finalist announced ruefully that the run might literally be a "race to the death."

The Soviet Union made its debut to the Winter Games. The competition was televised live for the first time, and after dominating the sport since its inception, the U.S. Bobsled team won their last medal, a bronze.

Snow Fall

January 19, 1956 - Wichita Falls - Memorial Auditorium

Wichita Falls Memorial Auditorium

Through San Antonio, Galveston, Beaumont, and Austin, the Hank Snow tour received outstanding acclaim. Always a big draw in the South, Hank Snow now faced an audience divided in its loyalties. Part of them came to hear his famous voice, and a good majority came to hear the young upstart.

On the fourth night into the tour, the troop hit an ice storm. For three days they played South and East Texas cities that stayed relatively balmy even in January. Thursday night's show ran in Wichita Falls, where nothing stopped the cold Oklahoma air from blasting through the very marrow of your bones. "Black ice," invisible ice hiding in the grooves of the pavement, covered the roads surrounding the city and lured unwary travelers into tailspins.

In separate cars the troop assembled at the Memorial Auditorium, exchanging harrowing tales of ten- and twelve-hour drives fishtailing the entire length of Highway 281. Scotty and Bill appeared together, but Elvis decided to drive on his own.

Elvis idolized Hank Snow, but the older singer definitely did not return the sentiment. The previous May, Parker had managed to talk Snow into letting Presley travel with the show. Parker and Snow shared a contract from way back, making them more of a partner relationship than manager and musician. Legally it could even be argued that according to their contract, Hank Snow owned part interest in Presley. Snow threw him at the bottom of the bill, more as a favor than anything else. It was his show; he could afford to be generous to unknowns.

But since then, the little brat's popularity had grown so much that no one on the schedule wanted to play before or after him, which left not much in between for the other performers. The kid was bad for the country music circuit. He had to go.

Five minutes to curtain and Elvis still hadn't arrived. Hank Snow chained smoked through his rage, demanding to know when Parker's precious singer planned to make his appearance. Parker sent Bill Mack and his band out first. Their enthusiasm left much to be desired. Snow paced, stubbing out butt after butt. Convinced that Parker had intentionally planned this scene by telling Presley the wrong time, Snow watched Mack and company file off the stage. Some of the crowd chanted, "we want Elvis" and the sentiment quickly

Scotty Moore. Wichita Falls, January 1956

Bill Mack and Bill Black. Wichita Falls, January 1956. Courtesy of Elsie Medlin

gained momentum through the throng.

With one last searing look at Parker, Snow stubbed out his last cigarette and strode onto the stage to face what had once been his audience just four months ago. His band dubiously filed in behind him. Snow began with some old favorites, but the teenagers booed. His band members glanced at each other nervously, but their lead singer chugged on, seemingly oblivious to the increase in the negative volume. Snow picked up the tempo and played a popular score. They booed louder. He played on, determined to get through his set, if only to get backstage and grab Parker by the throat.

Suddenly the air filled with bright flashes of copper. Someone threw a handful of pennies at the musicians. Take your money and get off the stage, it said loud and clear. Like lemmings, other teens followed until the air filled with waves of copper shrapnel, drilling Snow and his band. The song stopped dead as the musicians turned their backs to the stoning. Snow strode off the stage, dragging his band with him.

With the colossally bad timing usually only seen in sitcoms, Elvis appeared in a flashy red jacket. Whew, what an ice storm; that road is a killer; what's everyone looking at?

Snow grabbed Parker by the arm and propelled his "partner" into a dressing room. "I want that little son of a bitch fired" echoed through the halls, but the crowd couldn't hear; they had returned to their "we want Elvis" chant.

No problem, just hand me over your shares in the boy, Parker returned smoothly.

Snow refused, but it hardly mattered.

E. and Bill in Wichita Falls. Courtesy of Elsie Medlin

Shares or no shares, he never saw a dime of Presley's earnings.

Now for a little salt in the wound, Jimmie Rodgers Snow, Hank's son, thought Elvis was the greatest thing since sliced bread. Jimmie co-billed with Presley on numerous occasions and maintained a friendship, even when his father sued Parker in the sixties for equity lost over Elvis.

In February 1956 -
Senator Harry F. Byrd urged the southern states to resist the enforced school desegregation that the Supreme Court mandated in its 1954 Brown vs. Board of Education of Topeka, Kansas decision.

Ladies and Gentlemen, Elvis Has Entered the Building

April 9, 1956 - Wichita Falls - Memorial Auditorium

After the January Hank Snow tour fiasco, Parker booked Elvis for another show in Wichita Falls through Bill Mack. But this time, the ad read, "The Elvis Presley Show." No more second banana for his star.

Parker called Mack to make the arrangements. Hang posters on every telephone pole, stuff them in every store window, plaster them on people's forehead if you have to, he told him. "Advertise Elvis, Mack." Parker told him. "Advertise him until people get sick and puke, and then sell them a ticket." So advertise him, he did. No record remains if the city of Wichita Falls suddenly had an outbreak of nausea that week in April.

A sellout crowd awaited the Hillbilly Cat. The auditorium buzzed not only with young boys and girls, but a substantial number of rockin' grannies as well. Charlene Arthur and Bill Mack warmed up the crowd with the kind of music they came to hear, then made fast their escape, just in case any aerodynamic coinage happened to be revving on the runway.

When Elvis stepped onto the stage, the roar of several thousand voices made Oklahoma teeter on the map and sent aftershocks into Arkansas. No more high school gigs or mill openings; Elvis had arrived, literally and figuratively.

Elvis worked the crowd, allowing his unintentional charm and sensuality to join the wild clothes and haircut as part of his standard costume. The audience, in turn, pitched a frenzy that enervated the singer. He gave them 110 percent and they absorbed it all like energy sponges. Not satisfied with just a photograph, they leapt on the stage and attempted to extricate very personal souvenirs. The

He's really cookin' now. Elvis tears up the Wichita Falls Auditorium. Courtesy of Carol Lloyd

normally introverted Presley laughed it off . . . nervously.

After the last notes rained down on the upturned faces, Elvis sprinted backstage in such a good mood, he slapped one lovely lady on the rump. She scooted past him with a glance at Bill Mack standing in the wings. As Elvis passed Mack, he suddenly had an attack of conscience.

I hope I didn't offend her, he mentioned to the promoter.

I don't know about her, but that's my wife, Mack replied dryly.

Elvis blushed, looked at the floor, then with a sheepish smile, continued to the dressing rooms, where old friends awaited.

Teenage DJ Jay Thompson meticulously arranged the reels on his recorder. As the organizer of the Hillbilly Hit Parade on Breckenridge radio KSTB, Jay attempted to interview the artists that he spun at his station. People loved to hear the human side of their favorite singers, and the musicians loved the exposure. So many requests for "Heartbreak Hotel" lit up his phone lines lately that Jay thought an interview with its crooner would be just the ticket.

Bill Mack gave Jay a special backstage pass under the table. Parker usually demanded that all publicity run past his eyes first, but Mack had other obligations. Parker might be an integral part of the ol' boys network, but he

Jay Thompson and Bill Black, Breckenridge 1955.
Courtesy of Jay Thompson

E. and Jay Thompson (right) Breckenridge 1955.
Courtesy of Jay Thompson

revolved totally outside the DJ's network, a who's who club that moved mountains in those days. Like a fifties version of the game Six Degrees of Kevin Bacon, everyone in the music industry was related to each other through Elvis with no more than six connections.

Game 1:
1. The "Hillbilly Hit Parade" on Breckenridge station KSTB, currently run by **Jay Thompson**, originally prospered under the guidance of its earlier host, **Sid Foster**.
2. **Sid Foster** booked Elvis for **Breckenridge** several times.
3. **Breckenridge** is where **Jay Thompson** first met **Elvis**.

Game 2:
1. After **Sid Foster** left the Hillbilly Hit Parade, **Ben Hall** took over the show.
2. **Ben Hall** later moved to KDAV in Lubbock, where he wrote "Blue Days, Black Nights" for **Buddy Holly** to record for Decca.
3. **Buddy Holly** played opening act for **Elvis** for one of his Lubbock performances.

Game 3:
1. **Bill Mack** booked Elvis for the **Wichita Falls** show with Hank Snow.
2. Elsie Medlin attended that same **Wichita Falls** show, but she was actually from **Stamford**.
3. In her excitement, **Joyce Thompson**, Jay's wife, grabbed Elvis's shirt at the show in **Stamford** as he entered his car. (Elvis replied "Honey, I may need that," and she let go.)
4. Jay Thompson, **Joyce's** husband, interviewed **Elvis** in Wichita Falls.

April 9, 1956 Interview with Elvis Presley and Jay Thompson

Well now, country-and-western fans of our Hillbilly Hit Parade, this is an interview we're gonna give you with Elvis Presley. It's taken from the Municipal Auditorium up in Wichita Falls, Texas, where we were last night. Elvis played a big show. I think many of you were familiar with that. In fact a lot of you were up there.

We're gonna ask Elvis some questions, let him tell you straight because I think you'll get more out of it that way, and I know that each and every one of ya' are just waitin' to hear him talk.

Elvis boy, we want to first ask you how old you are?

Uh, I'm twenty-one, sir.

You're twenty-one years old. Sureheart, you got a few months on me, I'll tell you for sure. Tell us, before you got in this music business, what were you doin' for yourself?

I was drivin' a truck.

Drivin' a truck.

Yeah, I was a . . . I was a. Yeah, uh-huh. (laugh)

Was that back in Tennessee?

Yeah, it was back in Memphis where I live now. I was trying to say I was learnin' to be an electrician.

You decided to stick to truck drivin', huh?

Well, I was drivin' a truck and I was studyin' to be an electrician too, see?

I see. You got all mixed up in this crazy music business and that tore the electrician deal all to heck.

Tore the electrician and the trucks all up.

Tell us, how did you get your first break, or to make your first record with Sun Records?

Well, I went into Sun Records and there was a guy in there that took down my name, told me he might call me sometime. So he called me about a year and a half later, I went in and I made my first record "That's Alright, Mama."

Yeah, and from there on, why, we know a little about what happened 'cause those things been on the turntables like nobody's business.

How'd ya' get your start on the Louisiana Hayride? What brought all that about?

I went down there, as a, just to try out, more or less. And, I went down there once, and I went back again couple weeks later, and uh, the people they . . . they . . . they seemed to kinda go for my songs a little bit. So they gave me a job down there.

So, from then on you was a regular? You're not with the Hayride anymore, are ya'?

No, Last Saturday night was my last night down there.

Last night with the Hayride. How'd you pick up these boys, Scotty and Bill, you known them for a long time? They live there around yeh'?

Well, they live in Memphis, but I never . . . I never knew 'em until we made our first record.

That right?

Yeah.

Well, tell us . . . so what ya' doin' now, just makin' personal appearances 'round the country? Is that what you're doin'?

Yeah, we just tourin' the country, different place every night.

Different places and working TV shows and this and that, whatever the occasion comes. Elvis, you made a screen test. Can you tell us the result of that now?

Uh, yeah, w-w-we got a seven-year contract with Paramount Pictures. We'll have a movie coming out. I don't know when, but we start making it in June. So, some movie with Burt Lancaster and Katherine Hepburn called The Rainmaker.

Yeah, we'll be looking forward to that as I know all our listeners will and everything. I got a kick out of that on the Hayride last Saturday night, I'll tell you for sure. El, anything else in particular you wanna tell us before we break this little interview up?

Well, I'd like to tell you that I sure appreciate all the spins you've been give'n me.

You really helped me a lot and I'd like to tell you how much I appreciate it, and all the wonderful people that have been writin' in, buyin' my records and comin' out to our show, because that's sort of really what makes anybody is the people, you can make 'em or break 'em.

Well, I'll tell ya' for sure, they sure go for your style, I'll tell ya' for sure. Because, we get the cards and letters every day. We play the records. Incidentally, your new album's just takin' over our Hillbilly Hit Parade. That thing's going like a storm.

That's good and I'd like to tell you it's been a pleasure talkin' to you and I'll be seein' you again real soon.

We'll be looking forward to it. Thank ya'.

Parker saw red. He laid down the law that from then on, interviews would only be granted with a written consent with a hefty royalty check stapled to it.

Remember when...

showers were considered such a waste of water that all civilians took baths? The freestanding tubs with sloped-backs and slippery rounded floors made bathing one of the earliest X-treme sports.

The Rainmaker Washes Out

April 10, 1956 - Lubbock - Fair Park Coliseum

Between January 20 and April 9, Elvis took a sabbatical from Texas touring. Instead, he concentrated on satisfying the Elvis demand in other states, honoring his RCA recording contract, and practicing for a fledgling movie career.

"I Forgot to Remember to Forget" finally gave him a #1 place in the national charts with "Heartbreak Hotel" fast on its heels. At RCA, Elvis's status moved from "gee, I don't know, boss. Did we make the right decision?" to their most profitable recording artist.

Elvis, Scotty, Bill, and the rest of the "Elvis Presley show" toured the east coast, Florida, and the Carolinas. Elvis collapsed from exhaustion in Florida but promptly bounced back and toured Georgia and Virginia, against his doctor's advice.

After six performances on television's "Stage Show," the Jackie Gleason/Dorsey Brothers variety program, other more influential television shows clamored for the wonder boy. At the end of March, Elvis flew out to California (a mode of transportation that he avoided at all opportunities) to do the Milton Berle show and try a screen test for Hal Wallis, the producer of *Casablanca*. While in movie-city, he tried out for a nonmusical bit part for the upcoming flick *The Rainmaker*, playing opposite Katherine Hepburn and Burt Lancaster for his first acting attempt. (No pressure there!) Paramount signed him for a seven-year contract and offered him the part in *The Rainmaker*, but Parker told him to skip that one for a better role. Meanwhile, Paramount loaned him to MGM for *The Reno Brothers* which began production in August.

Elvis hopped back on the airplane and soared back to Texas, where a two-week tour of screaming teens and befuddled press awaited him.

Remember when...

Korean veterans returning from service filled the universities and kept the high school graduates struggling to meet the rapidly accelerating grade point curve.

★ ★ ★

10,000 Flock To Hear Rock N' Roller

Singer Elvis Presley Gets Wild Reception From Fans

By KEN KENNAMER

Elvis Presley, a dynamic rock 'n roll singer who appeared in Lubbock less than 18 months ago for $75, picked up $4,000-plus in a return appearance Tuesday - turning Fair Park Coliseum into a bedlam before two screaming audiences totaling 10,000 persons.

Presley is a 21-year-old singer from Memphis, Tenn., with long sideburns, a ducktail and a delivery that, at its peak, makes Johnny Ray look like slow motion.

And Tuesday night he turned Fair Park Coliseum into an amphitheater where the thousands of screaming, screeching, clamoring-for-more fans put on an act themselves seldom seen in Lubbock.

Jim Crook, assistant manager of Lubbock Chamber of Commerce, said Tuesday night that the Coliseum would seat 5,500. But during Presley's performance, there were almost as many standing as sitting. Crowds filled the back of the auditorium and the aisles, and ringed the platform where Presley performed. A full house watched the second show.

Twice during Presley's show, mobs of teen-agers pushed through the locked doors behind the platform, before police could stop the flow and re-lock the doors.

How can you describe his performance? And can it be called a performance or a production?

Voices Not Similar

He's been described as Johnny Ray with the St. Vitus dance, but the voices are in no way similar.

In fact, you heard very little of his voice Tuesday night. As soon as he would sing a few bars of a number, he was greeted by wails, screams and swooning acts that brought back memories of Frank Sinatra's hey-day.

"Heartbreak Hotel," "I Got A Woman," and "Blue Suede Shoes" literally brought down the house as did every gymnastic movement of his body.

20 Policemen on Hand

He wasn't mobbed, thanks to 20-or-so policemen on hand, unless you consider being surrounded by teen-agers wanting him to sign a picture, a slip of paper, their forehead, their arm - "sign your name on my arm and I'll never wash it again" - as being mobbed.

But as Presley put it, "I'm not mobbed until they start getting my clothes. They've done that in several places - last night in Wichita Falls, in fact."

What's he got?

Ask the fans.

Marlon Brando With Voice

"What's he got? He's got everything. He's Marlon Brando with a voice - and what a voice."

That was one of the thousands of teen-agers who pushed close to the platform where Presley was raising the dust with one of his western renditions.

Another said, "Man, he looks and acts just like one of us crazy mixed-up kids. Only when he gets up steam, he blows it off."

"Don't he look cool, Man, don't he look cool!"

"Why do we like him? Man, are you crazy? Why did we like James Dean? Why do we like Marlon Brando?"

Get Scornful Look

But mostly when you ask "What's he got?", you only get a withering, scornful look in return.

What's he got?

Ask his manager, Col. Tom Parker.

"I started managing him last year. You see what he's doing now?"

What's he got?

Ask Presley himself.

"I don't know what it is, but I sure hope it doesn't stop. I just sing."

That latter statement could be ranked with the understatements of the year. Presley doesn't just sing.

He sings - in a shaking, wavering voice that somehow manages to remain strong and give off emotion.

Beats on Guitar

He beats a guitar. You couldn't say he plays a guitar, he beats it.

He emotes. His face mirrors the words he's singing. Not the grotesque patterns that characterize Johnny Ray, but a more subtle display.

He moves. And how he moves. After a chorus or two of singing, he backs away from the microphone and shakes, rattles and rolls. He does a shimmy, a shake - everything that caused burlesque to be banned on Broadway.

He Gets Results

He gets results. His fans will tell you he's not a passing fancy, not a craze. And they point to his ever-rising record sales, his increasing fan clubs, and his latest achievement, a seven-year contract with Paramount Studios in Hollywood.

Presley announced the signing of the contract Tuesday. He said his first picture would be called "Rainmaker," and he would be starred with Burt Lancaster and Katherine Hepburn. He's scheduled to begin work on the picture in June.

In his dressing room between shows, Presley still couldn't get away from his following. The fans, oblivious to the dressing and undressing members of the band, leaked through police at the doorway to get pictures, autographs, or just to look.

He signed autographs on pictures, notebooks, paper, arms, legs and foreheads.

And he talked some too.

"One show out there sure takes it all out of you. A doctor told me I'd be better off doing manual labor for eight hours a day."

"What about the draft? Well, I figure it'll be another six months at least before I get drafted."

A young teen-age girl at his elbows squealed out, "Drafted!" O, Elvis, you don't mean they're going to draft you."

Presley turned on the grin and said, "I imagine so. After all, I'm just a normal, healthy American boy."

Which brought on more squeals.

The draft question had come up along with a query about a rumored club being formed by disk jockeys in a South Texas city. The club was to be called "Let's Draft Elvis Presley" club. Presley had never heard of the club.

Col. Parker had something to say on the subject of Presley's being drafted.

"I don't know whether they'll draft him or not. He's got a nervous condition, you know."

And so it seems that Elvis Presley has everything. One thing he has for sure. He has fans in Lubbock.

- Lubbock Avalanche Journal

Panhandle Refugees

April 13, 1956 - Amarillo - Municipal Auditorium

Amarillo Municipal Auditorium

Halfway through the tour, Elvis's car started hacking and wheezing. Since he had to drive all the way from Amarillo to San Antonio two days later, Elvis decided to seek professional medical advice in Amarillo. He pulled the Cadillac into the dealership service bay and related the recurring symptoms to sympathetic ears. After some deliberation, the diagnosis handed down was that the car suffered from a serious case of run-into-the-ground syndrome, a condition commonly seen today among Dallas commuters and soccer moms but in those days, only exhibited by musicians.

Wincing, Elvis asked if they could prescribe something so it wouldn't suffer. They told him to come back that afternoon.

Killing time in 1950s Amarillo consisted mainly of eating and window shopping for oil derricks. After a few hours Elvis returned to the dealership to find his steed sitting outside smiling a big sloppy Cadillac grin at him. The rumor of the car's death was greatly exaggerated, it seemed. Elvis gratefully ran around to all who had worked on his baby and thanked them, handing them free tickets to that night's show at the Municipal Auditorium.

As evening approached, man and machine drove off into the sunset, literally.

Meanwhile, three busloads of high school students and their harried chaperone rolled into town from nearby White Deer High School. Everyone sat in their allocated seats, prim but excited. Each student clutched a sack lunch on her lap. The teachers knew that the auditorium probably would be crowded and the kids might not get their three squares that day, so they required each student to bring enough well-balanced sustenance to get through the evening, as well as their signed permission slip. The chaperones thought they had prepared well for the upcoming concert.

Four hours later the same bus rolled in the opposite direction carrying rock concert casualties. Red-eyed girls blubbered into their hankies, their medusa-like manes gyrating from frenzied hair-pulling sessions. "I like him so much," they sobbed hoarsely. Many of the girls tried to powder their war-torn faces. Several teens had hobbled back to the bus, their shoes victims of the mob. The last girl to dash on the bus before it departed frantically covered herself up. Victim of a "mob mugging," her squaw shirt got yanked off somewhere between "Heartbreak Hotel" and "Money Honey" and would be found several hours later by a janitor, who would shake his head and wonder what the world was coming to.

In the front of the bus the chaperone sat, her head in her hands, wondering how she would explain this to the principal. An Elvis Presley field trip seemed like such a good idea at the time. What went wrong?

The presence of a drummer was a sure sign of a crossover group. The country music world considered it the "devil's instrument." Amarillo 1956. Courtesy of Barbara Welz Burns

The First Relaxing Moment in Months

April 15, 1956 - San Antonio - Municipal Auditorium

San Antonio Municipal Auditorium

Direct from the Jackie Gleason show, but just before the Ed Sullivan show, the "nation's only atomic powered" singer (a marketing creation from the fertile brain of Colonel Parker) rocked on the brink of stardom, and the teens of San Antonio knew it even if their parents still scratched their heads.

Overeager promoters booked two shows at the Municipal Auditorium, relatively certain they could fill half the seats each time. They sold 12,000 tickets then had to do a manual recount to recheck their totals (no hanging or pregnant chads). Sure enough, 6,000 teens plunked down their hard-earned savings to see Mr. Presley for each show, and see him they would. Unfortunately, the organizers hadn't taken South Texas stubbornness into consideration.

During the afternoon show, a mere ten police officers manfully attempted to keep the lusty natives from bridging the orchestra pit and storming the stage. Hopelessly outnumbered, they hung on until Elvis finished his act and disappeared. For a moment the audience stood stunned waiting for him to return. Surely it wasn't over already. In a classic example of mass-telepathy, the teens tore around the building to the stage door.

Originally Parker had planned to erect a table just inside the stage door to distribute autographs. But when a girl in front fainted and had to be hauled inside to prevent a trampling, other arrangements were discussed. At 6 p.m. three thousand teenagers refused to budge from their spot. Elvis couldn't leave the auditorium, and the promoters began to contemplate how to get the masses out in time for the next onslaught.

At first Elvis waved to them from the window and signed a few autographs, but eventually he retired to the auditorium pipe organ, where he amused himself by pecking out chords to "Silent Night." Outside, fans chanted "We want Elvis!" But his attention was too diverted by his practice to even show them a leg, as he would in Florida. One young man did his Spiderman impression up the sheer auditorium wall and received an autograph for his daring attempt. Don't try that at home, kiddies. Elvis returned to his keyboard and concentrated on "Harbor Lights."

By 7 p.m. officers stopped playing Mr. Nice Guy and physically hauled the pining, chanting teens off the auditorium grounds. The young people rallied and prepared for an all-night sit-in if necessary. Elvis ceased to appear at the window and hope faded. The determined officers finally succeeded in herding the fans off the premises, just in time for the second show. They called in reinforcements to guard the stage for the evening performance and popped a few dozen Bayer, wishing it were something stronger.

Elvis on the other hand was delighted. He discovered that after a bit of practice, he could actually play one of those big church organs by ear. What a peaceful and productive afternoon it proved to be.

ROCK 'N ROLL STAR STIRS NEAR RIOT

* * * * * * * *

3,000 FANS STORM ELVIS PRESLEY'S DRESSING ROOM HERE

By Gerald Ashford
Staff Writer

Elvis Presley, the 21-year-old Memphis boy who has become the hottest thing in show business since Frank Sinatra's best days, narrowly escaped being torn to pieces - unintentionally, of course - by a mob of some 3,000 fans who laid siege to the stage door of the Municipal Auditorium Sunday afternoon.

This occurred after a matinee which was the first of two performances given here Sunday by Presley and a group of other entertainers, whose names don't matter. The total audience at the afternoon performance was around 6,000.

In the melee, one girl fainted and was taken to Presley's dressing room, where Presley and others, properly chaperoned, applied ice packs and comforting words. After a few minutes of this, Presley looked into her eyes and asked her how she felt.

"I feel wonderful!" was the inevitable reply.

The near-riot started when Presley's managers placed a table across the stage door and asked the young people in the crowd to line up for autographs. But the entire crowd then pressed against the door and the attempt had to be given up. Others were swarming through all parts of the Auditorium in a fruitless hunt for their idol.

When Presley made an appearance in a mezzanine window above the stage door, one young man climbed up the wall and succeeded in getting his autograph. A few other autographs were handed out through a small, barred window in the dressing room.

Presley, aware from previous experience that it would be impossible for him to leave the Auditorium just yet, then retired to the keyboard of the big pipe organ. He had never played any type organ before, but after picking out a few notes at random he launched into passable renditions of "Silent Night," "Harbor Lights" and other tunes.

"These things fascinate me," he said of the pipe organ. He sang in a church choir, not so long ago, in his hometown of Tupelo, Miss., where he lived until he was 13.

Pointing to the mob outside, a reporter asked, "Do you get this everywhere you go?"

"Well," Presley replied thoughtfully, "if I said yes I'd be braggin', but if I said no I'd be lyin'."

His manager chimed in to report, "In Amarillo they broke the windows."

Hordes of impatient teen-agers Sunday night stood their ground at the Auditorium, with growing cries of "We Want Elvis" as the singer finished his second performance here.

Presley brought in more than 6,000 fans at Sunday night's show, a few hundred more than at the afternoon performance.

A few managed to get backstage after the show to get autographs from the star, and hundreds of others ganged outside his dressing room.

Presley, a young man who seems rather ordinary until he launches into his act on the stage, made his first commercial recording in Memphis only 18 months ago. As recently as January of this year he attracted comparatively little attention here as a supporting member of the Hank Snow hillbilly troop.

His stage act consists in equal parts of singing, guitar playing and dancing, the whole being classified, if it can be classified at all, in the "rock and roll" category.

To an adult ear, all his songs sound pretty much alike, but he puts them over with tremendous verve and vitality, and keeps it up steadily for nearly an hour without visible signs of fatigue, even after he leaves the stage. Perhaps because of his youth, he shows no signs of the nervous tension or need for rest that is common to older performers who put forth even half as much energy.

- San Antonio Express

AGONY, SWEET AND COMPLETE

Atomic-Powered Elvis Presley Bombs S. A.

By BETTY SCHEIBL.

A gum-chewing, nonchalant phenomenon named Elvis Presley moseyed off to Corpus Christi Monday to see what he could do in the way of searing the souls of additional thousands.

Behind him he left tears, screams, wild applause, mangled emotions - in short, agony, sweet and complete. It was a traumatic experience this newly arrived singing star brought to municipal auditorium Sunday afternoon and night. Youthful sufferers to the number of 12,000 writhed through it in sheerest ecstasy.

Commented Elvis backstage, sipping a soft drink before the first performance:

"This is just a dream. It makes you feel good. I've got everything a boy ever dreamed of having."

3 CADILLACS

"Everything" to the fans doesn't mean exactly what it does to Presley - his three Cadillacs (the fourth on order), his sports car, motorcycle and new house in Memphis. It's something on an entirely different plane, and it's potent enough to keep teenagers standing in line for three hours to get in to see him and then hang around in hordes to catch the second show. Some fans were even determined to follow him to Corpus Monday. What's the passion for Presley?

Squealed one girl:

"Because he looks so mean!"

The boy with the socko scowl, who can say "Yes, ma'am" politely and bestow lingering kisses with equal facility, strolled onstage for the first time at about 4:30 p.m., following a string of western entertainment that included Wanda Jackson, Hank Locklin, Charlie Walker, the Farmer Boys, Leon Payne, the Texas Cool Cat and several others.

SINCE 3

The show had been rocking the house since 3 p.m.

Elvis, 21, an ex-truck driver was wearing a white silk jacket, black trousers and a blue satin shirt with a mandarin collar.

Diligent research uncovered that he sang "Baby, Let's Play House," "Heartbreak Hotel," "Long Tall Sally," "I Was the One," "I Got a Woman, "Only You," "Blue Suede Shoes," "Money Honey," and "Tutti Frutti."

You couldn't hear Elvis on the front row.

Uproar exploded each time he looked as though he might open his mouth. A flash of white teeth from Elvis, a loose-hipped slur of dance steps, a Brando-like gaze from soulful blue eyes, and the floor vibrated with 6,000 stamping feet, whistles shattered the air.

Cries of "Look this way, Elvis" and "Here, over here!" drowned Elvis out. Lipreaders jumping out of their seats in the vicinity of this reporter obligingly supplied the song titles.

ATOMIC POWER

Presley is billed as the "nation's only atomic powered singer" and the program says his specialty is "a peculiar brand of western bop."

That may or may not be true. I didn't hear him.

But visually from across the footlights he comes through like the midnight express. He kicks, slinks, shimmies and gyrates.

At times he resembles a man who is desperately wrestling his way out of a particularly confining batch of saltwater taffy.

Ten policemen were on duty inside the auditorium for the

Presley show. Seven of them were down in front when the star came on, holding back the crowds (mostly girls) that threatened to surge across the orchestra pit and up on the stage.

Earlier the floor between the first row and the pit was a sea of full skirts as Elvis worshippers crouched and crawled into position cameras at the ready. They had to move back.

WE WANT ELVIS

After the show a throng estimated at 3500 jammed against the west stagedoor entrance, chanting "We want Elvis!" Plans to sign autographs from a table inside the door were abandoned when one girl fainted (she was dragged inside and revived by a policeman with an icebag and Elvis) and others burst into tears.

Presley waved to the screaming crowd from an upstairs window. One enterprising boy climbed up the shrubbery and won an autograph. A few autographs had been dispensed earlier to girls from Dallas and Austin representing the state's Presley fan club, largest in the world with 3000 members.

One girl who said it was her birthday was rewarded with a long kiss. Others got brotherly busses on the cheek, pats on the cheek, pats on the shoulder and squeezes.

At 6 p.m. the mob had not thinned sufficiently to permit Presley to leave the auditorium. He amused himself at the organ, calmly running through "Silent Night," "Harbor Lights" and several other tunes while the teenage public pined outside.

REAL GOOD

He plays by ear, used to sing in the choir in his native town of Tupelo, Miss., feels "real good" when he gets three or four hours sleep a night, never gets excited over anything, except maybe the fact his "Heartbreak Hotel" has just sold 1,000,000 records. He is under 7-year contract to Paramount.

Has he had any proposals since his rapid rise to fame in the past six months? Replies Presley

"I'd hate to say yes 'cause I'd be conceited, and I'd hate to say no 'cause I'd be lyin'."

If diplomacy counts in show business, Presley should be up there in the front ranks for some time.

- **San Antonio Express**

Some Things Never Change

April 16, 1956 - Corpus Christi - Memorial Coliseum

Corpus Christi Memorial Coliseum

Fame and fortune attacked Elvis with a vengeance, but still he hadn't changed all that much (except for a rumored nose job while he auditioned in California). On the way to his April concert in Corpus Christi he forgot to stop for gas and ran out halfway to the port city. He thumbed his way to the Coliseum in which 6,000 teenagers anxiously awaited to tear his clothes off.

You know, you can take the boy out of the country....

Rock 'n' Roll Shows Outlawed

CORPUS CHRISTI (AP) - "Rock 'n' Roll" shows were outlawed at Memorial Coliseum and Exposition Hall yesterday. The move came after more than 6,000 teenagers attended the Elvis Presley show Monday night. Many parents and some teenagers called the show "vulgar."

Building manager Tom David termed the show and others like it a contributing factor in juvenile delinquency.

Variety, a show business trade journal, recently featured a report on "Rock 'n' Roll Dynamite" and called it a phenomenon producing mass hysteria among youngsters.

No violence broke out at the local show. Police were stationed at the hall during the performance.

- Corpus Christi Caller Times

Know What I Mean Jellybean?

April 17, 1956 - Waco - Heart O' Texas Coliseum

Hillbilly, then rock-a-billy, then rock 'n roll, the media couldn't keep up with the names of the music types as fast as Elvis changed them. No longer the "Hillbilly Cat," he was now referred to by the dazed press as "the King of Rock and Roll." "Rock and roll," once literally a slang obscenity, now became adopted by the media as the perfect term for the strange, thumping-beat music Elvis and his contemporaries strung out like sausages.

Elvis impersonators popped up all over the country. Men, even women slicked their hair back in a D.A. (duck's *butt*) hairdo. Elvis was the King of Cool and everyone wanted to be him . . . except Elvis.

Heart O' Texas Coliseum in Waco

Shortly before he was to go on stage at the Heart O' Texas Coliseum, Elvis Presley, the new 21-year-old king of the nation's rock n' roll set, sat in a darkened Cadillac limousine for an interview—well hidden from the sight of nearly 4,000 screaming, squealing teenagers who were on hand to welcome him Tuesday night.

All the hep cats were there

and not enough fuzz (cops).

Out in the stands and on the floor, his audience of idolizing teenagers did all but hiss and boo to rid the stage of a group of other hillbilly entertainers and bring Presley out behind the microphone that he handles more like a limp blonde than a mechanical gadget.

Still Elvis made them wait . . . and he stared out at them, half-scared and half-unbelieving.

Then with some sort of spasmodic movement, he turned to talk about himself.

"What do you want to know about me, honey?"

"Elvis, have you any idea at all about just what it was that started the girls going crazy over you?"

"No, I don't. I guess it's just something God gave me. I believe that, you know. Know what I mean, honey? And I am grateful. Only I'm afraid. I'm afraid I'll go out like a light, just like I came on. Know what I mean, honey?"

Presley has a way with that "honey" business. When he talks, he looks straight ahead or sort of dreamy like in no direction at all. Then he turns with that "know what I mean, honey?" His face is close, real close, right in your face almost.

"When do you start making your first movie, Elvis?" (Everybody calls him Elvis.)

"Oh, early in June, I think, because . . . ."

At this point he stopped talking and stared ahead into the crowd. He squinted his eyes, jerked up a pencil (which had no lead) and began scribbling on the dash of the car. Then he turned and said, "Huh, did you say something?"

"Elvis, when you start acting, will you keep the sideburns?" (The sideburns come down below his ears.)

"Oh, I don't know. It depends on what type of part they put me in. You know, I'm supposed to do Billy the Kid pretty soon."

"But Elvis, Billy the Kid has been done to the ground."

"Yeah, I know, but this time it will be different." The way he says "different" it really will be.

"Elvis, will you sing in your first movie?"

"No, honey, sure won't. Going to be in it with Katherine Hepburn and Burt Lancaster, and I won't sing. I don't want to, I want to be an actor."

Then he turns and stares into the crowd again, listens to one of the other entertainers singing and grins slowly.

"But Elvis, have you thought how unhappy all these girls are going to be if you stop singing?"

"Huh, what was that? Oh, I'll never stop singing, honey, never."

He was beginning to make me wonder if I knew what I was talking about, so I changed the subject.

"Elvis, I hear you walk in your sleep."

"Well, I have nightmares."

"What kind?"

"I dream I'm about to fight somebody or about to be in a car wreck or that I'm breaking things. Know what I mean, honey?" (I don't have any idea what he means.)

"Where are you from?"

"From Memphis, Tennessee."

"Oh, yes that's where all the hillbilly singers come from, isn't it?"

"Maybe so, but I'm no hillbilly singer."

"Well, have you typed yourself . . . I mean your type of singing?"

"No, I don't dare."

"Why?"

"Cause I'm scared, know what I mean, honey? Real scared."

"What of?"

"I don't know . . . I don't know. Know what I mean, honey?"

At this point, I thanked him for his time and started to make a beeline for the door. He grabbed my hand, sat there looking sleepy-eyed into my face, and fanned his long lashes while he said:

"Write me up good, will you honey?"

And he drove out to meet the hysterical adoration of young girls and boys whose emotions he has found are easy to stir up with a song.

- Waco Tribune Herald

Big Dog, Little Dog, Flop-eared Pup, Come on Team, Let's Eat'm Up

April 20, 1956 - Fort Worth - North Side Coliseum

Local cops didn't know how to control a mob of crying, agitated, semiconscious teenage girls, but Elvis did. From the makeshift stage on the North Side Coliseum rodeo grounds, waves of females rushed the stage only to be stopped in their tracks by the *Look*. Stunned, they stood there quivering, like dogs behind invisible fencing, stretching out their arms in a pining, supplication move only seen in melodramas.

Police watched the spectacle in awe and envy. If only that power could be bottled and packaged with the military issue riot gear.

The *Look*.

"I Was the One, Honey"

Fort Worth - North Side Coliseum, April 1956. Courtesy of University of Texas at Arlington

Hysteria Grips Soxers

Rock'n Roll Presley Evokes Raw Display

BY ELSTON BROOKS.

In one of the rawest displays of emotion for an entertainer since Frank Sinatra swooned his first bobby-soxer in 1942, a crowd of some 7,000 persons cried, grimaced and screamed for guitar-twanging Elvis Presley at North Side Coliseum Friday night.

In a word, it was utterly fantastic.

Mass hysteria completely gripped the crowd - mostly teen-age girls - at two full house shows as it watched the drake-tailed young rock and roller who spiraled overnight from a $35-a-week truck driver to a show business millionaire.

And all at 21.

The audience patiently sat through a pre-Presley offering by various western artists, but by intermission one actually could feel the tension rising in the throng.

An animalistic roar split the coliseum as Presley sauntered on stage at last, guitar around his neck.

A cannon going off wouldn't have been heard when the shrieks rose as Presley pitched into his first number, "Let's Play House."

"Elvis, I'm going to die!" one girl shouted in ecstasy. She didn't.

"Elvis, I'm going to faint!" another threatened with closed eyes and clenched fists. She almost did.

* * *

PRESLEY CLOSED HIS EYES and began the sensual, almost vulgar swaying of his body that has made him a nationwide celebrity.

In a reaction better explained by Freud than *Variety* or *Billboard*, the girls collapsed on one another, moaning from side to side with closed eyes.

They screamed. Tears ran down their faces. They swarmed toward the stage.

Twenty policemen, imported for the Friday night show, shook their heads in amazement and ushered them back to their seats.

Forty girls from Dallas chartered a bus to attend the show. Two proudly displayed scars on their arms where they had carved the word "Elvis" with pocket knives.

Georgiana Blaylock, 16, and Dolores Orms, 16, both of Thomas Jefferson High School in Dallas, said their mothers called them "idiots" for carving their arms.

"I've done it four times - the latest one today," Georgiana said with a sigh.

"I've only done it twice," pouted Dolores.

As Presley moaned and swayed through "Heartbreak Hotel," "Blue Suede Shoes,"

"Long Tall Sally," "Only You," "I Was The One, Honey," and "I've Got a Woman," there was even a 3-year-old boy mimicking him from the first row.

Earl Lloyd Bright Jr., whose parents live at 609 Crosby, came to the show with a child's guitar, and strummed and swayed along with the star.

The Brights' other child, 20-month-old Laura, clapped her hands to the rock and roll music while sucking a bottle.

* * *

WE WISH TO GET ONE thing on the record this morning. Regardless of his act on the stage, Presley isn't the Marlon Brando-James Dean type some have reported him to be.

He's a polite, well-mannered young man who says "sir" to every question asked, and who is tremendously humble at his fabulous success.

He doesn't wear motorcycle boots and black denim trousers. Instead, he was expensively attired in a lavender sports coat, black dress pants, a flashy sports shirt and black loafers. He wears his sideburns long and there's a bit of a duck-tail to his hair, but apparently the kids like it that way.

Today he's the hottest new item in show business. His recordings of "Heartbreak Hotel" and "Blue Suede Shoes" are writing their own tickets on the Hit Parade. Next week he opens in Las Vegas at $20,000 for 14 days. He's just signed a seven-year contract with Paramount Pictures.

His tour manager estimates this year he'll clear $500,000. "Two years ago," Presley said in a backstage interview, "I was making $35 a week driving a truck in Memphis. Man this is the greatest thing that ever happened to me. It's a dream come true."

He says he's always "sung this way" since he first picked up a guitar at the age of 12.

His break came two years ago when a company decided to press a record of his after hearing a home recording.

- Fort Worth Star Telegram

"Just remember this. Don't go milkin' the cow on a rainy day. If there's lightning, you may be left holding the bag."

— E. P., Houston 1956

In June 1956 -
Congress passed the Federal Aid Highway Act, which allocated 33.5 billion dollars to build the first interstate highway network.

Nowhere To Run To

Elvis and the boys leaped from the frying pan of the Texas shows into the cold embers of Las Vegas, where the older sit-down crowd shrugged their shoulders through his antics and loudly asked the waitress if they could get another Harvey Wallbanger.

And bring another Pink Lady for the missus. And could you tell that kid to keep it down; I'm trying to talk here.

He suffered for two weeks, the only bright moment coming from a teenage matinee, and then returned to Memphis to find his home besieged. All through the day and night, young people with nothing better to do surrounded the house he bought his parents in April, stared in the windows, collected grass as trophies, and filled the lawn like a scene from *Return of the Living Dead*.

Elvis had appeared again on the Milton Berle show in June, the Steve Allen show in July, and the first of three Ed Sullivan shows in September, despite Sullivan's vow that he'd never allow that obscene boy on his show. Elvis sang "Love Me Tender" to fifty-four million people, and now they all showed up at his parents' house to fulfill his request for affection.

By October nearly every warm-blooded human being in America recognized the face of the Memphis boy. There was no turning back now.

In October 1956 -
Angry at the communist seizure of their farms, the people of Hungary revolted against Russia's regime. Khrushchev poured tanks and troops into Budapest and the surrounding countryside. Thousands of Hungarians were killed or sent to prisons in Russia, and over 100,000 fled to noncommunist countries as Russia set up a puppet government.

The next month a brawl between the two countries began during a water polo match at the Melbourne Olympics and quickly led into a full-scale riot when the spectators joined in. Several forces of Melbourne's finest broke up the battle.

A Day Which Will Live in Infamy

October 11, 1956 - Dallas - Cotton Bowl, Texas State Fair

Step right up ladies and gentlemen to the greatest show on earth. Not the Barnum & Bailey, but definitely a three-ring circus. In the far ring 26,000 heaving, hyperventilating teenagers from every corner of the Southwest descended on the State Fair in a parade of American-made cars. Some drove from as far away as Florida, and all were fueled by a frightening combination of caffeine, adrenaline, and sleep deprivation. They blocked all highways leading to the Cotton Bowl in a three-mile-long yelling, hanging out of cars honkfest. South Dallas traffic came to a dead stop as kids ran back and forth between the flying tailfins of halted cars. A wave of impromptu Chinese fire drills provided entertainment.

1951 Publicity shot of the Cotton Bowl. Courtesy of Dallas Public Library

In the near ring the press corps jockeyed for the scoop, shoving fan club members and other media members aside to get the best story. Elvis's money? His movie plans? The Fort Worth subpoena? All topics served as fodder in the battle of radio versus newspaper dominance. Competing camera flashbulbs from fan club members and reporters sizzled the air at the press conference until Elvis told one girl, "Careful with them flashbulbs, honey. You'll burn mah sideburns off."

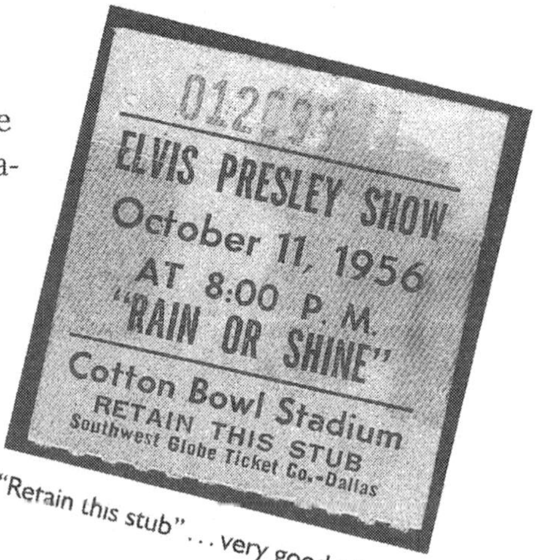

"Retain this stub" . . . very good advice.

BUT ROCK 'N' ROLL QUARRY BUSINESS

CLEBURNE Oct. 11 (AP) - The Cleburne office of the Agricultural Stabilization and Conservation program had a request for tickets to the Elvis Presley show in Dallas Thursday night.

The caller said Elvis was appearing at the Cotton Bowl and the ASC must have tickets since cotton was part of its business.

Rock and roll tour programs didn't exist when this Souvenir Photo "Albun" was first distributed. Bummed at the spelling mistake, Parker had them reprinted.

In the center ring the King and his attendees entered the circus with stealth and diversionary tactics. Even his own people didn't know the game plan. The strategy proved necessary as thousands of eagle-eyed scouts scrutinized every gas-guzzling land yacht that drove into the State Fair, hoping to discover Elvis hiding in the glove compartment.

There he is! A delusional girl pointed and hundreds of rally cries answered as fans madly scrambled to the Cadillac. Inside, a terrified corn-dog hedonist screamed and hit the gas to escape the invading army.

That wasn't him, they exclaimed as exhaust fumes engulfed them.

Musicians astern! A boy shouted a few minutes later.

Several cars passed through the gate, faces glued to the windows in fascinated terror.

Ah, that's just the warm-up band. The crowd moaned and reposted their sentries.

In the escaping car Sherry

asked them if they wanted to back him up permanently and they enthusiastically agreed, the quartet attended all the concerts. Even though they recorded most of his RCA hits, including "Hound Dog" and "Heartbreak Hotel," very few people recognized their faces. They escaped the sentry post without being frisked.

Six carloads of Hawkins kids parked in upper-Slabovia and hiked to the stadium.

Elsie Medlin and Jane Giles stepped off the bus from Stamford. Flashing their fan club passes, they hustled past the disgruntled press and into the stadium backstage, the wire-cutters safely hidden in Elsie's purse. They heard through the fan club that a fence would surround the field and thought they'd come prepared.

At a quarter till, the outposts were abandoned and all forces converged in the stadium. Twenty-six thousand rustling, nervously giggling souls waited for a single human being to enter their sights. Sherry Davis and the other singers flashed across the stage, playing songs that all heard, but no one listened to. All eyes and ears stood guard for the man.

At 8:55 an excited hush fell over the audience. One hundred police officers manned the wire war-zone fence. The thump of several

Davis and Tom Diskin crawled through the gates and into the guest parking lot. When Sherry's boss at the Big D Jamboree asked her if she wanted to play warm-up for Elvis's concert, he didn't mention anything about human roadblocks. A big crowd, he said. He never mentioned that the entire population of Texas would be attending.

Gordon Stoker and the Jordanaires rolled onto the grounds. Ever since April, when Elvis thousand hearts echoed off the walls. The lights dimmed and a spotlight pierced a white convertible as it emerged from the tunnel and circled the field, a side-burned man clearly visible in the glow. Thousands of blue flashbulbs cracked and popped behind the eight-foot-high fence like enemy artillery. The car stopped next to the stage on the 50-yard line, and the "weirdly handsome" Elvis stepped out and waved. A mighty soprano-banshee roar rolled like breakers over the field. The Saxons were invading!

Elvis leapt onto the stage, joining Scotty, Bill, and the Jordanaires. The tidal surge abated slightly, waiting for him to say something, but he tossed his head back and laughed. An earsplitting crescendo of squeals slammed against the entertainers. They cranked into "Have Some Fun Tonight," and the screams of 26,500 hysterical girls deafened the musicians. Elvis didn't even bother to strum the guitar; no sound would have been heard over that tumult anyway.

At first he sang with his fingers in his ears, vainly straining to hear the music played a couple feet away, but then he abandoned the fruitless effort. If he couldn't hear the music, no one could hear the music. Elvis belted out his tunes, heedless of tone or tempo. He jerked his head and twisted his body in time to

"He ripped into 'Have Some Fun Tonight,' complete with the gyrating pelvic motions which are best described as a cross between an Apache war dance and a burlesque queen's old-fashioned bumps and grind." - Tony Zoppi. Dallas 1956. Courtesy of Steve Bonner

"You ain't never caught a rabbit and you ain't no friend of mine." — E.P. Dallas 1956

the music in his own head. Behind him, Scotty and Bill desperately watched Elvis's hip thrusts to keep the tempo, prompting Scotty to remark in later years that they were the only band "directed by an ass."

He played all the faves, not that anyone could hear them. At the end of his thirty-five-minute stint, he jumped off the stage and crawled around in the grass singing, "You ain't nothin' but a hound dawg" in his electric green sports jacket, navy pants, white bucks, and black-and-gold striped cummerbund. (Pretty reserved wardrobe choice, you'll agree.)

When he hopped into the convertible and disappeared back through the dark tunnel, the fans gasped in disbelief. Gone? He was gone? He just got here. It can't be over.

Oh, but he was and it was.

Elvis and Nick Adams, the actor friend (and Parker spy?) he'd met while filming *Love Me Tender*, retired to their room at the Stoneleigh, a quiet hotel on the outskirts of town. Thousands of saddened souls trod home, already reminiscing about that time he brushed his hair back or twitched his leg in just a certain way.

Half of Dallas attempted to find him that night. Hotels were ransacked and evidence traded, but no Elvis. The fan club set up a spy network to scour the city faster. Now, if you were an Elvis, where would you be hiding? The investigations continued into the wee hours of the morning, but only two groups found him. Elsie and Jane caught up with Scotty and Bill and wheedled Elvis's location out of them.

Meanwhile, a Dallas lawyer (using his own network) tracked him to the Stoneleigh but didn't know which room. Good breeding prevented him from pounding on every door, barely. He brought a girl to the concert that he badly wanted to impress. For twenty bucks he bribed two hotel workers to admit that Elvis occupied a room upstairs. The workers looked the other way as the two stowed away in the service elevator to the correct floor then disappeared unobtrusively.

No security flanked the halls, but neither was there a sign that said, "Elvis snores from this room here." The two slunk to the floor and waited for indications of movement. Surely someone would want a late night Tastee Freeze run.

Elvis and Nick Adams came around the corner and almost tripped over the couple. In his opening argument, the lawyer introduced himself and told Elvis the girl just had to see him. He prepared to present People's Exhibit A, a pair of Cotton Bowl tickets with lipstick marks on them, but Elvis settled out of court.

Come on in, he told the couple. Shrugging, they complied.

They all gabbed for about an hour. But when it became time for the ice cream run, the lawyer stood, dragging his girlfriend with him. As the lawyer propelled her through the door, she grabbed the doorframe and asked Elvis for an autograph.

I'll give you something better to remember me by, he told her, and gave her a whopper of a kiss. Dazed, she stumbled backwards out into the hall and completely forgot to get an autograph.

Is Fort Worth It?

As a sideshow to the three-ring circus of the Cotton Bowl, the reporters gleefully observed a Dallas County deputy sheriff attempting to serve Elvis with a summons. The papers in the hand of W. R. Pike alleged that Elvis broke a contract with R. G. McElyea of Amusements Enterprises, when he didn't play a promised Fort Worth performance. (Parker organized all the concert dates. Elvis knew nothing about them until his manager told him where to play and when.)

A car sped up the tunnel surrounded by police escort, their sirens blazing, and the deputy sheriff lay in wait for his prey. A man in a green jacket jumped out of the car, and Pike pounced ... on the wrong man. Gene Smith, Elvis's bodyguard and decoy, refused the summons as it didn't have his name on it. Gene hustled down the tunnel, Nick Adams at his heels (probably to warn Elvis). Pike saw Nick and suspected he was actually Elvis in a really amazing disguise (especially since Elvis stands a head taller than the actor and had his dark hair slicked back instead of curly and blonde). Pike vaulted down the tunnel after the two men, where he slapped the papers at the actor, who promptly refused them.

A few moments later Elvis emerged at the top of the tunnel in another car with Parker. Pike sprinted back up the incline and attempted to hand the singer the papers, but they fluttered to the ground. Neither man attempted to pick them up. Parker hauled the deputy sheriff with him to work out the legal details and allow Elvis to get on with the show.

After they left, Elvis told Nick, "I turned my ring around. I thought that guy was going to jump on you."

In the end Parker told North Side Coliseum that Elvis would play two more shows for them before December as previously arranged. When the original dates with Fort Worth were scheduled, Elvis still received a pittance in royalties. So quickly did his popularity grow, that now he received thousands of dollars for each appearance. To actually play Fort Worth again would cause them to lose money. These concerts never occurred. After considerable hemming and hawing, Parker bought out the contract, as he did with the Louisiana Hayride.

Remember when...

your parents wouldn't let you swim in pools in the heat of the summer for fear that you'd contract polio and become crippled? Salk's polio vaccine was released in April 1955.

Elvis Has Bodyguard Like Presidential Party

BY ANN JONES.

Besides a few government wheels like the President, Elvis Presley is probably the most closely guarded man in the United States.

At least, Kenneth Moore thinks so after traveling with Presley through Ohio during the singer's recent personal appearance tour.

R. G. McElyea and Moore, who handle programs at North Side Coliseum, booked Presley for shows in Toledo (the place where the singer was attacked by a jealous husband), Cleveland, Troy, Ohio, and Louisville, Ky.

"He has to be guarded or he would be torn to pieces by the fans," Moore explained.

All manner of security measures are taken to see that the rock 'n' roll idol isn't mobbed by his admirers. But, somehow, things slipped up a bit when Presley was attacked by the man from Toledo, who claimed that his wife carried the singer's picture in her billfold instead of his.

Most of the time, however, Presley's bodyguards manage to keep him in the clean, Moore said.

"But he hates the word 'bodyguard' and prefers to call them traveling companions," the Fort Worth man added.

When Presley arrives in a town, he is always registered into a hotel under a false name. Arrangements are always made in advance to have police in the hall outside the singer's hotel door to keep out any fans who might get that far, Moore pointed out.

Before Presley leaves his room, someone always scouts the halls and hotel lobby to see if any crowds are waiting to swarm him. Then, the rock 'n' roller uses the back service elevators.

When he gets ready to leave for the auditorium where he's to sing, Presley jumps into a police car, a waiting cab or an ordinary car. The teenagers would spot his Cadillacs and wait for him, Moore explained.

After the show, Presley rushes to a waiting car to get out before his audience realizes he's gone.

THE PRESLEY BODY IS GUARDED LIKE GOLD

Numerous arrangements are made with police, hotel officials and various other persons before the singer ever gets to town, Moore said. All this detail work is done to keep fans away from him as much as possible.

As an added precaution, Elvis is always surrounded by his entourage and various business associates, including manager Tom Parker, a publicity man, an auditor, Gene Smith (a cousin and constant companion), actor Nick Adams, a friend and "traveling companion," and Presley's automobile driver, who also doubles as a bodyguard.

This is only part of the group that goes with Presley wherever he appears, Moore said.

"Privacy is one thing he has little of."

Moore said that the teenagers' hero would "like to mix and mingle with his fans" but that it was just too dangerous. "You can't be sure what might happen if a mob got loose at him."

Although the Presley troupe goes to untold trouble to keep their movements secret, Moore recalled, news of Presley's whereabouts always leaks out.

"Those teenagers have an espionage system that the FBI should take lessons from," he smiled.

This could be one reason that Presley sometimes displays nervous symptoms.

"He's like a caged tiger sometimes," Moore noted. "He gets awful keyed up and just walks the floor. But, take it from me, he's one of the nicest guys you'd ever want to meet."

And, for all of Presley's fans in the Fort Worth area, Moore has a bit of encouragement.

Despite rumors circulating that Elvis would not be back in Fort Worth for another show, take it from Moore, "he's still scheduled to appear here."

Details of exactly when haven't been worked out yet but it will probably be after the first of the year, Moore said. "There's a very slight chance we might arrange something for the middle of December. I doubt it, though."

So, adorers of Elvis, mark it in your date book — Presley, North Side Coliseum, early 1957.

- Fort Worth Star Telegram

Moore Gets in Way

Oh No!--or Hooray! Elvis to Be Delayed

BY ANN JONES.

Elvis Presley fans - read this and weep!

It looks like he won't be appearing in Fort Worth any time soon after all. Presley originally was scheduled to appear in North Side Coliseum in November or December. He has another date left on a contract made with the coliseum early this year.

Then it looked like his appearance couldn't be set until early 1957. Now word comes that he won't be here until some time after March, Kenneth Moore of the coliseum said.

Moore went to Shreveport this week-end to meet the rock 'n roller and his manager, Col. Tom Parker, in hope of setting an early date for Presley's show here.

Elvis is due to be on Ed Sullivan's television show Jan. 6. Then he begins work Jan. 14 on his second movie, this one for Hal Wallis Studios. That will take about 10 weeks and Presley hopes to have a short vacation when the film's completed.

If the Army, which is rumored breathing down the singer's neck, decides it can do without him a while longer, EP probably will hit Fort Worth in the spring.

FROM LOW BILLING TO A PEDESTAL

It's a funny thing what a year can do. In June of 1955, Elvis was billed about fourth on a program of hillbilly and western singers during a North Side Coliseum show.

He turned up again in January 1956 at the coliseum as a supporting act with Hank Snow. But, this time, his following was growing and he stole the show from Snow, who vowed he would never share the stage with Presley again.

In April, The King of Wiggle returned and his fans went wild.

All in less than 12 months.

Each year has its sinners and saints, its heroes and villains. Looking over 1956, it could best be termed the Age of Elvis.

To most oldsters, he's the sinner-villain, an object rating only hisses. To most youngsters, he's the saint-hero, worthy of limitless loyalty. To everyone, he's something you can't ignore.

So, our hats off to this guitar-plunking knight in blue suede shoes. What would we have talked and read about if it hadn't been for him?

- Fort Worth Star Telegram

The Morning After

The next day Elvis caught up on some much-needed sleep while the other singers car-pooled to Waco. He and Nick Adams piled into Elvis's beloved new Cadillac and trundled through Oak Cliff on their way to Waco. An entourage of two, Eddie Fadal and Elvis's cousin Gene Smith, followed. Since Elvis could now afford a car of his own, he enjoyed taking it for a spin whenever possible.

Halfway up Jefferson Street (the only way out of town), the Cadillac suddenly executed a hairpin turn. Fadal slammed on his breaks and swerved around him, spitting sentiments that described Elvis's family lineage. Elvis had spotted an army/navy store and decided to stop for a little shopping. The Cadillac docked in front of the strip mall, and Fadal patiently pulled in behind him.

The army/navy store didn't offer any choice selections in orange, pink, or purple, so Elvis settled on a couple of pairs of slacks, which would have fit him perfectly if he were an Aboriginal basketball player. The store tailor agreed to alter the pants legs more to scale. It would, however, take an hour or so.

Elvis continued shopping and found a truly killer motorcycle cap but nothing else of immediate appeal. He, Fadal, and Gene wandered next door to the Midway Café to fortify themselves for the upcoming two-hour drive with a bowl of chili or two.

E. and Eddie Fadal chowing on some chili at the Midway Café. If they got bored, they could always listen to some of E's records on the table jukebox. Dallas, October 1956. Courtesy of the Fadal Estate

With pinkies extended, yet. Midway Café - Dallas, October 1956.
Courtesy of the Fadal Estate

Barely had Elvis plowed through the kidney beans and scoped out a few jalapeños before an Oak Cliff reporter materialized next to the table and asked if he could take a few snaps. The fact that the restaurant owner was a buddy of the reporter surely had to be coincidental.

Elvis agreed to the photos as long as it didn't mean an interruption into his gastric foray.

The photo flashes attracted attention, and soon the restaurant overflowed with curious bystanders pointing at Elvis in the manner of zoo patrons in front of the tiger exhibit. Oh look dear, a rock 'n' roll singer in his natural habitat. He doesn't look that dangerous.

A photographer from the studio next door came over and begged Elvis to sit for a portrait. Always a pushover for a pretty face, he told her, "Sure honey, let me finish my chili."

True to his word, after dining on the epicurean cuisine, Elvis strolled next door. The lady photographer arranged the seat, arranged him, and then arranged her camera, in that order. She shot him, motorcycle cap and all (just a flesh wound).

When Elvis left the studio to retrieve his long-overdue hemming, he totally forgot about the photograph. His friend Eddie Fadal remembered however. Fadal returned to the studio and retrieved the photo. The photographer gave him the negatives and the prints but

The same motorcycle cap appears in pictures of Elvis for the next couple of years. Dallas, October 1956. Courtesy of the Fadal Estate

kept one for herself.

In 1958 when Elvis visited the Fadal family home during a weekend furlough from the army, he spotted the photo on the mantel. Curious, he asked his friend where he had gotten such a great shot. Fadal replied, "You remember that studio in Oak Cliff with the lady photographer?" If it wore a skirt, Elvis remembered it, and he remembered posing for the picture. Elvis took the photo off the mantel and signed his initials, as he did with his close friends. He returned it to its roost but continued to admire it. Out of all the photos that had been taken of him during the years, Elvis remarked often that this one was his favorite. (Probably because it made him look so hip and James Deanish.)

In October 1956 -
When Johnny Cash's song "I Walk the Line" made the Billboard Top 40, the "Grand Ole Opry" requested that he adorn their stage. His appearance on this nationally broadcast radio show launched Cash's career into the Country Hall of Fame.

Devil in a Pink Dress

October 12, 1956 - Waco - Heart O' Texas Coliseum

Some people heard Elvis on the radio and thought, "Wow, great music, I think I'll buy his record." Kay Wheeler heard Elvis on the radio and thought, "Wow, great music, I think I'll start his fan club."

Undeterred by the fact that Elvis neither lived in Texas, nor was born there, Kay decided that she would start the *National* Elvis Presley Fan Club in Dallas. After all, if not her, than who, and if not Dallas, then where? Tupelo and Memphis already had their chance. The spunky fifteen-year-old attacked her chosen goal with a concentration that would have won her a gold, had she competed in the Olympics.

Aware that towns like Stamford were jumping on the local fan-club bandwagon, Kay concentrated her efforts on the big-money round. She bought all the pink stationery she could locate and used a system of correspondence to convince all the other fans clubs that they needed to affiliate with her club in order to be recognized nationally. As incentive, Kay distributed membership cards, advertisements for upcoming shows, and photographs she had coerced from Elvis' manager of the time, Bob Neal. Her little club began to grow in popularity in direct proportion to the fame of her idol.

In January 1956, when Elvis's new song "Heartbreak Hotel" made its debut, Kay called KLIF Radio in Dallas and badgered her favorite DJ to play it in an unending loop. He succumbed to her request because it appealed to his sense of humor, and because he liked the

Kay Wheeler reads up on her favorite celeb. Courtesy of Kay Wheeler

song. The DJ even gave her fan club a plug as an excuse for his lapse in judgment. Just the mention of a fan club sparked such an enthusiasm in the listening audience that the mailman had to haul her family's take in a wheelbarrow. Thousands of letters poured in and Kay very dutifully answered them all on pink stationary, the official color of Elvisdom.

Meanwhile miles away, Elvis's new manager, Colonel Tom Parker, heard the broadcast and his ears perked as he did the simple math.

National Fan Club = hoardes o' females @ $1.50 per show
+ at least 30 cents a record
+ $1.50 per ticket in upcoming movie

= $$,$$$,$$$

E. and Kay in San Antonio.

Colonel Parker proffered a polite invitation to the young lady for the April 15, 1956 show in San Antonio and the April 20 show in Fort Worth. She politely accepted then hung up the phone and shrieked. Not just any old invitation, Parker promised her access to the most coveted spot in the country, Elvis's dressing room . . . p roperly chaperoned, of course. By this time her idol had become a national icon known to young and old alike. The shivering, screaming multitude that pressed up against the barricades as she walked by was proof that other young people were finally displaying the same healthy obsession that she diagnosed in herself a year before. It took 'em long enough. But still, it is nice to be validated once in a while.

When Kay arrived at each auditorium, she found that true to his word, Parker left the necessary passes to get her through all the checkpoints, which was beginning to resemble entry into East Berlin. Kay found herself waltzing past a bedlam of frenzied, fenced-off enthusiasts. In an instant, she discovered how Queen Elizabeth must have felt during her coronation a couple of years previous. That club card definitely had its advantages.

By the October '56 shows, all of her hard work paid for itself. Kay was granted special passes to meet Elvis at the Dallas Cotton Bowl performance, one of the little perks that came with the job included invitations for anyone she wanted to drag with her. Kay experienced no lack of interested parties. Because she was such a devoted daughter (or because she had to live with them), Kay invited the female contingency of her family, who had long since become Elvis enthusiasts. Not surprisingly, they all accepted. Even her mother attended, carrying a portrait of Elvis she had painted for him as a present.

Kay and company marched past the police barricades and right into the dressing rooms. News reporters played second fiddle to the fans. During the so-called press conference, they had to throw their questions over the heads of the bobbing ponytails of a select number of fan club representatives.

Channel 5 in Fort Worth tagged Kay as a prospect and interviewed her about the Cotton Bowl show. Afterwards they followed her closely, apparently hoping that she would lead them to a secret assignation with Elvis (they should have been following Elsie and company back to the Stoneleigh). Instead Kay led them to the Park Cities Lion's Club, where she had been elected to explain the rock and roll phenomenon to a bevy of blue-hairs over tea.

Everyone has their limit, and Waco was Kay's. After the riot of sobbing hysteria, agitated fits, and body mutilations that hallmarked the Cotton Bowl performance, Kay found herself quite unprepared for the courteous reception by the Waco audience.

They applauded quite happily between songs; they even yelled his name. But not a single soul threw herself in front of moving vehicles or carved his name into her arm with a pocketknife and colored it with burned matchsticks. No one got arrested. Not one single person in the audience succeeded in ripping off Elvis's clothes, not even his shirt. Kay was incensed.

Seething, she told a reporter that Waco was "the squarest town in America" and that they should be honored to have the King dirty his feet on their red clay... so to speak. Kay was not what you would call a word-mincer. Amused, the Associated Press picked up the interview and sent it to all its news outlets nationwide, and her 15 minutes of fame extended for another week.

The next day Tom Diskin, Parker's right-hand man, pounded on her door. The Colonel was quite cheesed, it seemed. Most of Waco had been amused by the article and her

Posing. Waco 1956. Courtesy of Jimmy Willis

More posing. Waco 1956. Courtesy of Jimmy Willis

This posing thing has really gotten old. Waco 1956. Courtesy of Jimmy Willis

outrage; the Colonel saw a public relations nightmare looming on the horizon.

He sent Diskin to demand that she retract her statement and apologize, tell everyone that she had been misquoted or suffered from an early onset of Touret's syndrome, or something. She squared her shoulders and told the man point blank, "I will not. Parker doesn't own me." Parker's reaction to this statement has never been documented (which is probably just as well).

Despite the tax on her time and jealous boyfriends (lots of that going around), Kay continued to organize star-struck teens into a national lobbying force that could have taught Washington a thing or two. Often acting as an official spokesperson, Kay always responded in the same demure style that the Waco newspaper found so amusing. When it was suggested by a reporter during one interview that maybe Elvis had run his course and interest in him was dying, Kay replied succinctly, "Elvis will last as long as there are women around." A truer word was never spoken, Miss Wheeler. You go, girl!

He didn't mind posing with the stagehand, though. Waco 1956. Courtesy of Jimmy Willis

In Waco with Bill Black peeking in the corner. Courtesy of James F. Jasek

Positively hit it off with the stagehand, in fact. Waco 1956. Courtesy of Jimmy Willis

It's a jungle out there!! E. doesn't seem to agree with Miss Wheeler's assessment of the Waco audience. Waco 1956. Courtesy of Jimmy Willis

Waco High on Elvis' 'Hound Dog' List

DALLAS, Oct. 14 (AP), — The national president of an Elvis Presley fan club doesn't have time to work — she's too busy taking care of her 10,000 club members "who really go for that boy."

Right now Kay Wheeler is fighting mad about the way Waco treated "the idol of teen-agers everywhere."

"You know that place Elvis sang in holds 11,000 people and only 5,000 showed up to hear him sing," the 17-year-old black-haired girl said. Presley appeared in Waco during the weekend.

"Why they ought to be flattered he came to that town. Waco is the squarest town in America. Why those people just sat on their hands while he sang."

"I'm going to do something about that town," Miss Wheeler said.

"And Elvis was obviously affected by the way they treated him there," she said.

More than 26,000 persons turned out to hear the rock 'n' roll sensation when he appeared at the Cotton Bowl in Dallas.

"He told me Dallas was one of the biggest triumphs in his career and he gave me lots of credit for it," she said.

The Dallas girl graduated from high school in June but has not gone to work or to college because her fan club keeps her busy.

Does she get paid for devoting her time to Presley?

"Why, no. Who would want money for doing that," she declared. "Heavens to Betsy, no, I don't get paid."

She said, "He never writes me. He's just too busy."

Miss Wheeler's club got its big boost when she wrote an article for a movie magazine titled, "I Flipped Over Elvis."

"I got 1,000 letters a week after the article came out and since then I've got 500 a week. I've got 10,000 club members in the country — 4,000 in Houston alone. But that Waco, I don't have a club in that city."

She's met Presley four times in Texas but "every time I get near him I can't say the things I'd planned on saying. I just kind of flip when I see him. At the press conference in Dallas he said 'Hello, Kay,' to me and I almost flipped. Oh, he's the most."

It was suggested to her that perhaps the country was getting tired of Presley.

"That's the biggest idiotic statement I ever heard," she said.

What about Frank Sinatra?

"Who?" Miss Wheeler asked.

- Waco Herald Tribune

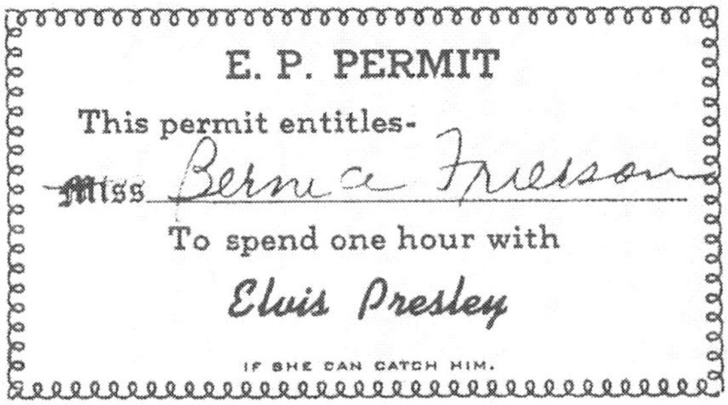

Lucky Bernice. Another marketing triumph brought to you by the folks who gave you the Elvis lunchbox. Waco 1956. Courtesy of the Fadal Estate

Quick, someone call an exorcist. Waco 1956. Courtesy of James F. Jasek

Yes, But Do You Have the Elvis Action Figure with the Kung Fu Grip?

October 13, 1956 - Houston - Sam Houston Coliseum

Step right up folks and get your Elvis merchandise for tonight's show at the Sam Houston Coliseum. Forget those saddle oxfords and blue suede shoes. Anyone who is anyone will be wearing those one of a kind (or in this case, 50,000 of a kind) Elvis tennies, guaranteed to be genuine authentic reproductions, made out of 100 percent rawhide canvas. Those little canvases never gave their lives for such a good cause.

But wait, there's more.

Do you really want to impress Elvis with your sincerity? How about the Elvis hat, "perfect for fan clubs." When Elvis sings to a sea of upturned faces, he'll spot you immediately in the hat with the names of all his songs (mostly because you look like Gilligan).

But don't order now.

How can you claim to be totally dressed without your designer Elvis lipstick to match your Elvis inspired poodle skirt. The lipstick comes in six day-glow colors that'll get you noticed. Heartbreak Pink is a perfect choice for the time you tell your boyfriend you are going to the show with or without him. Boldly coat yourself in Hound Dog Orange while baying at your favorite singer. Or, try Cruel Red when writing your phone number all over the nearest Cadillac with Tennessee license plates. He'll be guaranteed to think of you then.

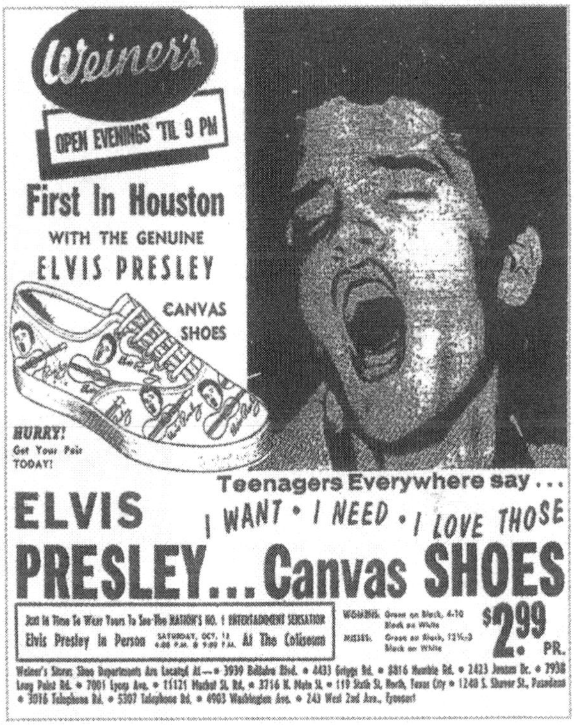

At the end of '55 Parker introduced a few Elvis trinkets at the concerts, mainly to keep the kiddies from extracting their own souvenirs off the singer's body. Tweens and teens snatched the knick-knacks up like rare gold coins. But by the Houston show in 1956, merchandising of Elvis products could have taught Disney a thing or two.

Once upon a time, lunch boxes or the occasional decoder ring advertised a favorite radio

For a low, low price, you too can get your own Elvis hat (foreground) to match your Elvis shoes. Courtesy of Sherry Davis

show, but that was child's play. Probably inspired by the brief but spectacular Davy Crockett craze, Parker ordered busloads of the Elvis goodies and made an unholy mint. Anything that had a surface big enough to slap Elvis's name on became fair game for Colonel Merchandising.

Elvis drinking glasses filled every cabinet, Elvis anklets and necklaces adorned his fans. You could use your Elvis overnight case to bring your Elvis PJs to the slumber party. Or use that Elvis ashtray when you sneak a smoke

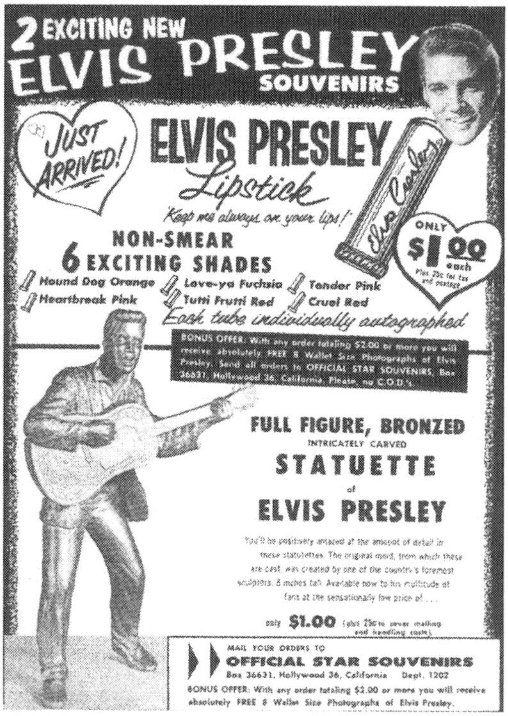

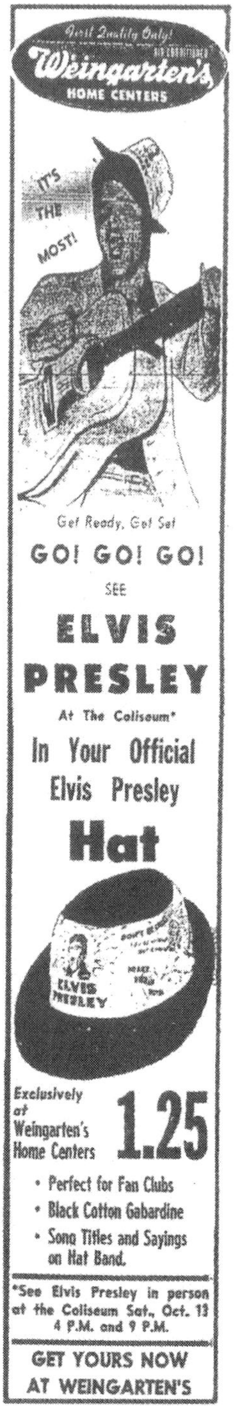

ELVIS PRESLEY ROCKS 'EM

8000 Teeners Scream At Self-Winding Singer

BY DICK DE PUGH
Chronicle Staff

The wails and screams of more than 8000 rock 'n' roll idolizers gave a tumultuous opening to the first show of the famed Tennessee playboy Elvis Presley, Saturday at the Sam Houston Coliseum.

The howling "hound dog" artist with his rhythmic accomplices were met with mob hysteria to open their two-performance stand here.

Presley's appearance was preceded by six variety acts to warm up the crowd into its frenzy. The circus prelude included one torch singer, two acrobatic acts, a comedian, a slack wire act and a quartet.

Swept into the Coliseum by a police guard, the greasy, sideburned hillbilly took to the stage an hour later.

Screams and lamentations kept up without relief for four minutes and 50 seconds.

He entered the arena like a wild calf and began his bellowing to the tune of his million-seller, "Heartbreak Hotel."

All that was heard of this number was the title. Screams from the crowd drowned out any other sound Presley could produce.

Three times he paused his panorama of bump and grind to plead with his audience to listen to him.

Deafening roars were the answers each time.

In the midst of the teenage tumult, a squad of 50 police officers, emergency corpsmen, and firemen were circulating the aisles to keep admirers from rushing the bandstand.

Elvis rolled and wiggled through "Blue Suede Shoes," added his hippy "oomph" to an agonizing rendition of "Love Me," and pulsated vigorously as he groaned his "Long Tall Sally."

Holding his hands to his ears, so he could hear himself, he wore his guitar slung around his neck, seldom striking a chord.

He rocked on his toes, pointed to kids in the audience and sang to them, and made a quick exit on a little number called "Hound Dog."

Toward the end of Elvis' second show, Saturday night, a hysterical teen-ager with a flowing pony-tail broke through the police line surrounding the stage and rushed her idol.

Police carried her back to her seat, but she had broken the ice.

Teen-age girls en masse clamored for Presley, and rushed the stage until the singer was whisked off in a waiting police car to his suite at the Shamrock Hilton Hotel.

Statistics: No one fainted. No one was injured.

- Courtesy of The Houston Chronicle

Elvis Says Faith Cause of Success

HOUSTON, Oct. 14 (AP) - Elvis Presley sprinted in a side door at the Sam Houston Coliseum yesterday, fled to a downstairs dressing room, kissed about 50 girls who were waiting for him, told reporters faith was responsible for his success, and went out on stage to give an afternoon show.

Surrounded by a phalanx of policemen, he ran to the microphone, his guitar slung over his shoulder, and stood there grinning while more than 8,000 fans, mostly girls between 12 and 17, screamed their deafening approval.

The yelling finally slowed down after almost five minutes.

Limber-limbed and hip-swinging, Presley faced a crowd of more than 8,000 at each of the two performances here. For all the noise, the audience generally stayed in their seats and Presley's manager said it was the "best controlled group" of the tour.

The rock and roll idol, unaware that he was to sing in the afternoon, arrived with a police escort some time after the show started. About 50 girls had been waiting in his dressing room for more than two hours, so he kissed each one of them.

"I believe in God," Presley said, explaining his success. "I advise young singers to have faith like I did. Everything happened so blame fast I don't know where I was yesterday or where I'll be tomorrow."

On the stage Oscar Davis, Presley's agent, was asking the crowd to sit down.

"Just remember," he said to relatively few parents, "it might be your child that gets trampled."

Statistics: no stampedes, no one fainted, no one was injured.

- Courtesy of The Houston Chronicle

in the boys room. Skirts, hats, shoes, scarves, key chains, statuettes, charm bracelets, notebooks, diaries, etc. all proudly bore the Elvis logo.

If imitation is the sincerest form of flattery, then Parker should have blushed with all the flattery. Other promoters promptly stole his idea to advertise their own groups.

So when you drive through that Taco Bell and buy your 72-ounce kidney buster of Dr Pepper in the collectible Flubber cup, you can say, "Thank you, Colonel, for giving the world more plastic tumblers that don't fit in my dishwasher." Perhaps if you listen really hard, you might even hear very faintly as you pull out into traffic, "No. Thank you."

Atom and Eve

October 14, 1956 - San Antonio - Bexar County Coliseum

Joe Strauss (a.k.a. Bexar County) Coliseum in San Antonio

If Waco didn't quite live up to Miss Wheeler's expectations, then San Antonio certainly made her smile. So many women lost their sanity that the San Antonio police department called out extra troops to the Bexar Coliseum to hold the banshees back. Arriving hours before the show, the quivering females stood on their chairs clutching each other, watching the bronco gate at one end of the old rodeo grounds, praying that it would open and reveal their god.

Just then the gate creaked open. A roar of screams erupted from the audience. Girls pulled out their hair and cried, wringing their hands in agony. The police grabbed each others forearms to form a human barricade against the surging tide. The bronco gate swung wide and a little man sauntered out with a broom and dustpan. He bent to pick up trash. The crowd drooped in disappointment. The grounds keeper continued his litterquest, oblivious to the tidal moan.

They continued their vigilance for their "atomic powered singer."

Eeeeeek, I'm going to faint! San Antonio, October 1956. Courtesy of University of Texas at San Antonio Institute of Texan Cultures

A man stepped onto the stage and 6,000 mouths opened to scream, but it was only the emcee. They slumped back in their chairs dejectedly.

We have a great concert for you this afternoon, the man told them.

(They applauded in general agreement.)

Tonight, Bexar County Coliseum proudly presents Elvis Pres... The emcee's mouth kept moving, but no words could be heard over the ear-splitting volume.

...lineup of great stars.

(Applause died; the thought of sitting through an hour of some other performer dampened much of the initial enthusiasm.)

And I know you'll treat them right, because they're all personal friends of Elvis.

(Wild applause. Any friend of Elvis...and so on.)

So, patiently they sat, applauding each country music act and secretly keeping an eye peeled in case Elvis accidentally stuck his head out from behind stage. A string of variety acts kept the venue hopping, but after an hour and a half, teenagers started getting the jitters. Ten minutes to atomic blast off....

THOUSANDS SCREAM FOR ELVIS

By CONNIE COLLUM
Teen-Age Editor

Thousands of fans screamed, sobbed or gazed in a stony trance while Elvis Presley bumped around a raised stage in Bexar County Coliseum Sunday afternoon. Paid admissions totaled 6,619 at the first of his two shows, in San Antonio Sunday.

Ninety percent of his audience were teen-aged and female, but one middle-aged matron on the front row watched him with starry eyes.

Sunday night's performance, before a similar audience, was a repeat of the afternoon "concert."

Elvis Wiggles

"He's wonderful," she said, "I don't see anything wrong with him."

Elvis, in black suit with white tee-shirt and bucks, stood straddle legged, wiggling his hips, as fans fell to their knees before him and beat their palms and heads against the floor.

"Ahhh, I want him. I want him," screamed one fan in a pink dress (Elvis' trademark is pink and black). Tears rolled down her cheeks. "I just want to touch him," she cried.

A girl collapsed on the floor. As police picked her up to carry her out, she struggled, ran, was recaptured and carried screaming out of view of her idol.

Fan Weeps

Another fan sat on the floor and wept throughout Presley's part of the show. "I like him so much," she sobbed.

Elvis was the calmest person in the Coliseum. Once, as he leaned limply over the mike, arm swinging loosely and hair hanging over his face, Elvis looked out at his hysterical fans and laughed. The screams grew louder.

"I'd like to do a song," he said.

Only the beat of the music can be heard over the cries of the audience, but Elvis can be seen - and the faster he gyrates, the more frenzied his fans become.

Fans Rush Stage

Several fans rushed the stage and were escorted out. One girl did not know her name. "Oh, oh, oh," she babbled incoherently, not taking her eyes off the stage, "I don't remember."

His appeal is indescribable they say, "I'm not here to find out what it is," one girl explained.

"He just makes me feel so crazy," squealed another, hugging herself.

Screaming was at its height and fans were pressing closer to the stage as Elvis finished his last number. He gyrated off the stage on the last notes of the song and jumped into a waiting car. The car left rubber streaks as it squealed out of the Coliseum. The escape took eight seconds.

Mob Dressing Room

Hundreds of screaming young girls mobbed the dressing room door chanting. "We want Elvis." They refused to believe he had gone.

Fifteen minutes after Elvis' departure, the coliseum proper was almost deserted. Two girls sprawled across chairs.

"We're gonna rest awhile, man, we're tired," they said. They were coming back for his 8 p.m. performance, they added.

Seventy-five of Elvis fan club members were at the Coliseum at 7 a.m. Sunday. Others arrived as much as six hours before the show.

Nine . . .

Had any marriage proposals in the last six months? "I'd hate to say yes 'cause I'd be conceited, and I'd hate to say no 'cause I'd be lyin'." - E. Presley. San Antonio, October 1956. Courtesy of Sherry Davis

Eight . . .

For the evening performance, Elvis swapped the green jacket of the afternoon for the more sedate black suit, white shirt, and white bucks. Courtesy of University of Texas at San Antonio Institute of Texan Cultures

Friends of Elvis

"We've been here cheering for Elvis," they said. Hundreds chanted, "Hey, Hey, Ho, Ho, Come On Elvis, Let's Go!"

Fans were asked to give consideration to the acts preceding Presley's appearance.

The audience cheered when they were told that the performers were personal friends of Elvis's and clapped enthusiastically for the hour and one half variety show.

Besieged by the press (each San Antonio High School sent reporters) in the dressing room before his appearance, Elvis was calm, friendly and cooperative.

"Really Nice"

"He's really nice," said a photographer.

He hugged fan club presidents and contest winner Marie Mendoza, Sharon Porter and Linday Windham, answered questions, posed for pictures and signed autographs quickly, then was rushed to the midst of his hysterical fans.

"I'm just doing the best I can," he said of his music. "I let each day take care of itself."

Of his success he said, "kind of scares you."

- Courtesy of the San Antonio Express

Seven...

The poetry contest winner.

Rhythm in Blues
dedicated to Elvis

I love your escapes
Which are some peoples debates
But who's complaining
It's you who's fame gaining.

Wherever you go,
Whomever you meet
There's always somebody
Who will be so discreet.

I just want to add,
That if I were to have,
But one singer to choose,
Surely you couldn't lose
For my only choice,
Would be your wonderful voice.

- a devoted, everlastingly happy, and
contented fan,
Marie Nilda Mendoza, age 18

San Antonio, October 1956. Courtesy of University of Texas at San Antonio Institute of Texan Cultures

Six...

Okay guys, just like we did in practice at the Cotton Bowl. San Antonio, October 1956. Courtesy of Sherry Davis

Five...

A one and a two and a... San Antonio, October 1956. Courtesy of Sherry Davis

Four . . .

"I'll be so lonely, baby. Well, I'm so lonely, I'll be so lonely I could die . . . " San Antonio, October 1956. Courtesy of Sherry Davis

Three . . .

"Oh baby, yes baby, whoo-oo-oo-oo baby, I'm havin' some fun tonight." San Antonio, October 1956. Courtesy of Sherry Davis

Two . . .

Long tall Sally has a lot on the ball, I can't hear this music at all. San Antonio, October 1956. Courtesy of University of Texas at San Antonio Institute of Texan Cultures

One . . .

"Well, it's one for the money, two for the show, three to get ready, now go, cat go!" San Antonio, October 1956. Courtesy of Sherry Davis

Blastoff!!

"At times he resembles a man who is desperately wrestling his way out of a particularly confining batch of salt water taffy." - Betty Scheibl, San Antonio, October 1956. Courtesy of Sherry Davis

Worst First Day on the Job

Sherry Davis's agent never discussed the finer points of mob maintenance when he hired her to open for Elvis Presley. The Fort Worth gal didn't know much about Elvis, since they revolved in different circles; she in old-time country tunes, and he in modern devil's music. Elvis had played the Big D Jamboree in Dallas several times, so he couldn't be *all* bad.

At the October 11 Cotton Bowl show, Sherry managed to pass her first survivor task without:

a. getting voted off the island,
b. eating a rat, or
c. ever meeting Elvis.

At 8 p.m. she attempted to quell 26,000 volatile rock 'n' roll she-cannibals by loudly pounding out nonstop hillbilly country music, all the while clicking her heels together and chanting, "There's no place like Fort Worth. There's no place like Fort Worth." After her set, Sherry vaulted off the stage before 52,000 handfuls of spare change took to the skies . . . two pocketfuls apiece. She caravanned with the rest of the troop to Waco for their performance the next night.

The mere 5,000 shrieking voices in Waco seemed positively like a warm-up after Dallas. Perhaps because the ad that hit the Waco newspaper proclaiming the big Cotton Bowl show didn't actually appear until the day after it actually occurred, the stadium remained half filled. Sherry slid through her set and retired to the hotel, bypassing the parties and preparing herself for a repeat performance in Houston the next night.

No sooner had she begooked her face and slid into bed, when an insistent pounding jolted her post-facial bliss. Sherry padded over to the door and cracked it open just a titch. Three psycho-broads burst in, their poodle skirts wringing in crisis.

Where is he? they demanded.

Where is who? she asked in confusion.

The girls looked under the bed, behind the drapes, in the medicine cabinet.

Where is Elvis? they demanded with the desperate tone of parents who just discovered that the last Furby sold an hour ago.

Well, he's not in the medicine cabinet. Annoyed, Sherry herded the room-jackers out into the hall. They promptly pounded on the door down the hall.

Where is he? she heard as she closed the door. (No need to bolt the door, however; crazed or not, people didn't walk into a motel room in the fifties without admittance. It just wasn't done.)

The next night in Houston, when the voracious predators tried to beat down her door for a little nocturnal search-and-seizure, she barred the entrance and didn't leave the room until the safety of the morning light.

On the road to their fourth and last show in San Antonio, Parker's right-hand man Tom Diskin asked Sherry what she thought about Elvis.

Her reply was noncommittal. He's a good showman, she said.

Yes, but what do you think about him personally?

I don't know. I've never met him, Sherry responded truthfully.

Diskin couldn't believe his ears, either because she as a female should have been throwing herself on Presley's feet, or because Elvis surely should have made moves on her by this time. Maybe the King was slipping.

Well, we'll just have to take care of that, Diskin promised.

Sure enough, when they arrived in San Antonio, Diskin took her over to Bexar Coliseum and barged into a press conference. He introduced Sherry to Elvis, who did a quick double take. Sherry strongly resembled Debra Paget, the actress in *Love Me Tender* Elvis had a crush on. After a couple of brief introductions, the press squeezed her out of their questions and eventually, the room.

That afternoon, while she prepared for the unscheduled afternoon show, a knock sounded on her dressing room door. She opened it to reveal Elvis, leaning against the door frame with his best 100-kilowatt "welcome to the show" smile. With a slow southern drawl, he apologized sincerely for the rush treatment at the press conference earlier and wanted her to know how much he appreciated her on the team. She thanked him politely and shooed him out of her dressing room, closing it firmly behind him, but not before he managed to plant a kiss on her cheek.

The bedlam of the San Antonio shows that day exhausted Sherry, but not enough to turn down Gordon Stoker's offer to take her to the Alamo. Though it was already closed, the Jordanaire knew she desperately wanted to visit the historic site, so prominent in Texan memory. So, they drove his Cadillac into old town and strolled the hibiscus-bordered paths, reading the plaques. When they returned to the car, one of San Antonio's finest stood sizing up the Cadillac.

"... Presley and a group of other entertainers, whose names don't matter." - Gerald Ashford, San Antonio Express. E. and the Jordanaires, San Antonio, October 1956. Courtesy of the University of Texas at San Antonio Institute of Texan Cultures

Is there some problem, officer? Stoker asked.

Is this your car?

Yes sir. (It doesn't hurt to be polite to the local constabulary.)

It has no license plates.

Yes sir. I can explain that. You see, we're with the Elvis Presley show and . . . well, the girls in the audience stole them. They steal anything connected with Tennessee. I guess they thought this might be Elvis's car.

Ah. The officer nodded in deep thought for a few moments, but apparently that explanation seemed bizarre enough to ring absolutely true, because he sent them on their way without a citation.

Actually, the women in the audience must have thought Colonel Parker's Cadillac might also belong to Elvis. They stole his license plates and wrote their phone numbers all over it in Heartbreak Pink lipstick. When fans besmeared Elvis's car, Parker had found the practice amusing, proving that the Memphis boy stood on the brink of true fame. Amazingly enough, however, graffiti doesn't seem so funny when the Cadillac is yours.

Parker tried to have it cleaned, but that Elvis Presley lipstick lived up to its "eminently kissable, won't wash off" hype. Heartbreak Pink and Hound Dog orange smudges detailed the expensive exterior. Elvis might have loved the color combination, but Parker didn't. He drove it to the nearest San Antonio Cadi dealership and traded it for a new model.

When Gordon Stoker and Sherry returned to the motel, they hung out by the pool and discussed Scripture. Both had grown up in fundamentalist homes. About the time Psalms appeared in their conversation, so did Nick Adams, swinging from Elvis's balcony, making chimpanzee noises, and wearing nothing but a smile. He dropped to the ground beating his chest and knuckle-galloped over to a hastily vacated chaise lounge. In ten strides Sherry had a motel door between herself and the missing link.

A few minutes later Gordon Stoker's apologetic voice called through the door. Elvis wanted to see her, did he? Well, maybe he does and maybe he doesn't. Completely cheesed, she stomped across the parking lot to give the singer a piece of her mind, possibly even the entire frontal lobe.

Elvis met her at the bottom of the stairs with a smile that could disarm a terrorist. Gently he took her resisting hand and gazed into her angry face with cocker spaniel eyes.

Nick has something that he'd like to say to you.

I'll just bet he does, Sherry thought. Parker probably heard about his little stunt already and is afraid she'll tell the press.

Sherry allowed herself to be led up the stairs. Elvis tugged her into a room where the now fully clothed Nick gushed a semi-sincere apology for his primal behavior.

I don't often meet *decent* girls, he remarked, shoving his foot deeper in his mouth. It's so nice to actually meet one.

Sherry threw him a verbal bone and turned to leave. When she reached the hall, Elvis slid into her path. He placed one nonthreatening hand on the wall behind her and when she didn't protest, closed the cage with his right.

Could you remain angry to this face? RCA promotional headshot from 1956.

He gazed into her eyes, body heat warming up the autumn air between them.

You're a good lady, he whispered.

She returned his gaze pointedly. Yes, I am. Her voice held no room for negotiation. Elvis straightened up as if she had just passed the final question on the Presley good-girl/bad-girl exam.

Well, don't ever change, he suggested. Without my faith, I wouldn't be where I am, he added.

And where would that be, Sherry wondered, looking at his introverted expression.

Elvis offered her a gentleman's arm, and she grudgingly accepted. They strolled to the balcony overlooking the pool. While they leaned over the railing and watched the lights ripple over the water, a drunken fan stumbled over to them asking if they had seen Elvis. He turned and looked the woman in the eye. No recognition lit her face. Without a word, Elvis pointed across the walkway and she wobbled off in that direction. A few minutes later the woman returned.

Hey, he's not there, she slurred.

I don't know how you missed him. He just went by on the way to the pool, Elvis told her, once again staring into her eyes for recognition.

Thanks mister, she breathed her 100 proof thanks, which almost toppled him over the railing.

What a handsome couple they would have made. Sherry Davis' recordings have been recently rereleased on the "Gals of the Big D Jamboree" CD. Courtesy of Sherry Davis

Elvis walked Sherry to her room and stopped at the entrance. He gave her a brotherly peck on the cheek and told her to stay sweet. She thanked him and started to swing the door around but noticed his feet. He wore crocheted booties made for him by one of the Jordanaires' wives. But at that moment his big toe stuck out of a little hole in the top.

Hey, nice slippers. She closed the door.

He's a Fightin' Man, He's a Lovin' Man, He's a 20th Century Fox

What could possibly be better than a live Elvis concert with 26,000 of your closest friends? How about his baby-face stretched across an eighty-foot movie screen? In November *Love Me Tender* released to theaters nationwide. The waiting lines for this boy-meets-girl, boy-loses-girl, boy-wins-girl-back-and-then-croaks film made the teenagers' parents fondly reminisce about the days of *Gone With the Wind* and the ten-mile-long lines it produced. Maybe that's why all of those parents allowed the entire teenage population of America to cut class and stand outside for hours in an unusually cold November, just to see the man who *Variety* announced had become a millionaire in one year.

The kids didn't grow cold, though. Memories of Elvis kept them warm. In Texas those recollections would have to keep them toasty for a very long time. The October 14 performance in San Antonio proved to be the last time he played in the Lone Star State for some fifteen years.

Early Fans Shake and Quake Just Like Elvis

BY ELSTON BROOKS.

A trembling, quaking, shivering and shuddering mass of females, known to science as Americana Presleyana, leaped from warm beds as early as 3 a.m. Thursday so they might stand outside a downtown building in 25-degree weather for 6½ hours.

You're old and gray, dad, if you can't figure out that the building was the Worth Theater where Elvis Presley's first movie, "Love Me Tender," opened at 9:30 a.m. Thursday.

There are only several thousand seats inside and 16 of the junior high set wanted to assure themselves of a seat once Mr. Sideburns began grinding his way across the Cinemascope screen.

They brought sandwiches secreted inside coats. Others stood shifts in the line while their partners got breakfast at the Worth Hotel.

Parents Delivered Them.

The weather bureau reported the 25-degree low was the coldest here since Feb. 5 when it dipped to 24.

What do the parents think about all this?

"They got out of bed to bring us down," shouted one exuberant girl proudly displaying a button reading: "Elvis Is Our Cause - Wow! What A Cause!"

Marcia Murdock, 14, of 3713 Winthrop, a William Monnig Junior High student, made her touchdown at the darkened box-office at 4:30 a.m., becoming the envied first in line.

Naturally, she wore a skirt with giant letters on it spelling out Presley's name.

Jimmie Ivy, 14, of 3909 Bonnie Dr., wore Presley socks and hat. She entertained the frozen throng by singing "Don't be Cruel," a la Elvis, while the other girls put in "bop, bops" at strategic points in the melody.

Louanne Worley, 14, of 7209 Garza Ave., decided to be adult about the whole thing.

Said she, with a stiff upper lip: "I already know Elvis gets killed in the picture. I'm glad I know. Otherwise I think the shock of seeing him die on the screen would make me cry too much."

Several in the line got misty-eyed at the quote, and the rock 'n roll dancing stopped for a few minutes. It seemed like a nice gesture.

There was a lone male in the crowd, too. Jackie Hunter, 12, a J.P. Elder Junior High student who lives at 1414 Grand was there also by 5 a.m.

"Heck, the boys like Elvis too," he said.

The girls had a multitude of answers to a reporter's simple question of "why all the fuss over Elvis?"

Multitude of Answers.

Samples: "He's cute."

"He understands our problems."

A short, piercing scream.

"I just want to get something out of my system."

A shocked sob, and a long sigh.

"Don't you like Marilyn Monroe?"

The last one stopped the interview.

- Fort Worth Star-Telegram

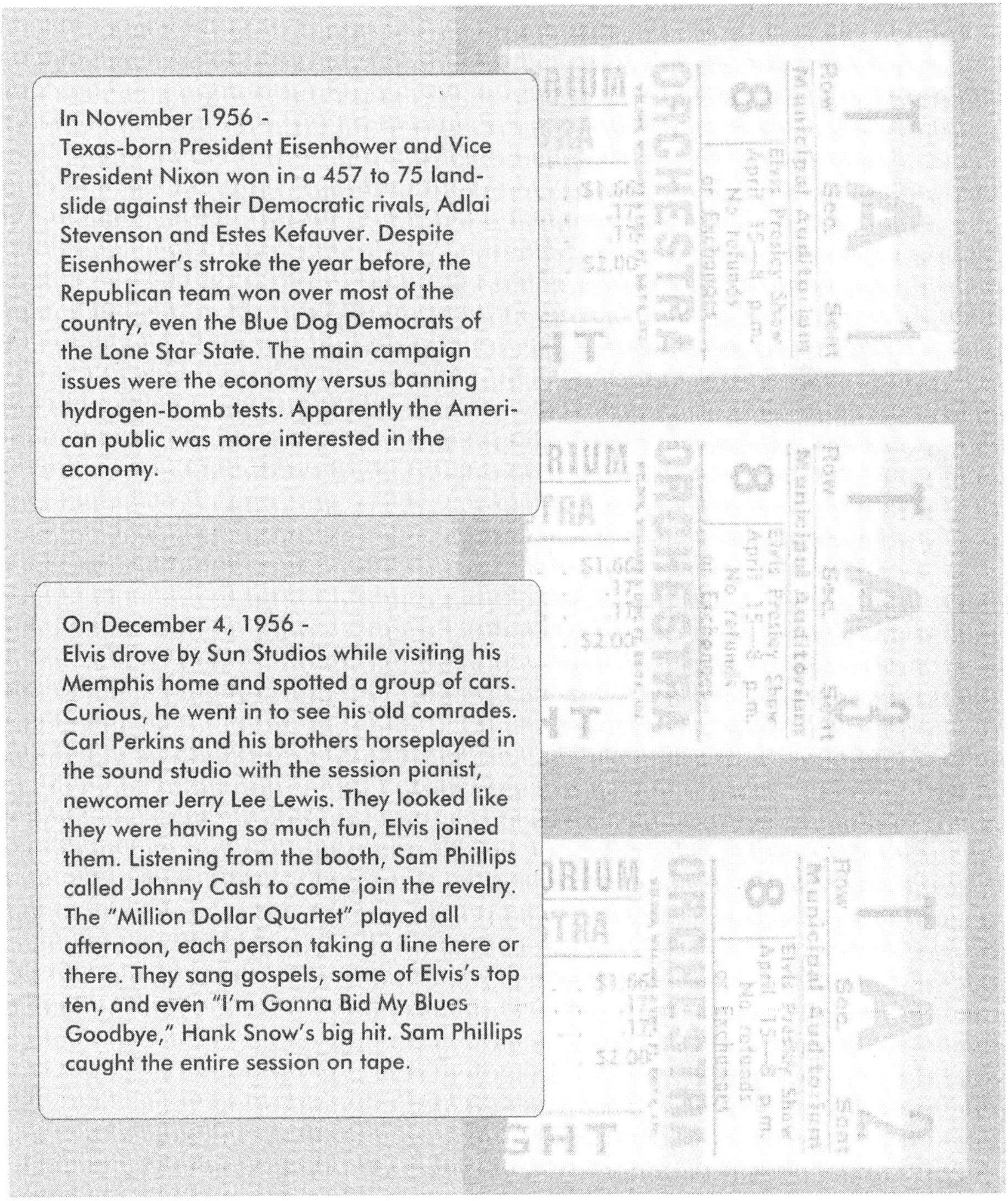

In November 1956 -
Texas-born President Eisenhower and Vice President Nixon won in a 457 to 75 landslide against their Democratic rivals, Adlai Stevenson and Estes Kefauver. Despite Eisenhower's stroke the year before, the Republican team won over most of the country, even the Blue Dog Democrats of the Lone Star State. The main campaign issues were the economy versus banning hydrogen-bomb tests. Apparently the American public was more interested in the economy.

On December 4, 1956 -
Elvis drove by Sun Studios while visiting his Memphis home and spotted a group of cars. Curious, he went in to see his old comrades. Carl Perkins and his brothers horseplayed in the sound studio with the session pianist, newcomer Jerry Lee Lewis. They looked like they were having so much fun, Elvis joined them. Listening from the booth, Sam Phillips called Johnny Cash to come join the revelry. The "Million Dollar Quartet" played all afternoon, each person taking a line here or there. They sang gospels, some of Elvis's top ten, and even "I'm Gonna Bid My Blues Goodbye," Hank Snow's big hit. Sam Phillips caught the entire session on tape.

Courtesy of the Fadal Estate

Uncle Sam Wants Him Too

The most famous haircut in history outside of Sampson and Delilah. Elvis gets his ears lowered. Fort Chaffee, Arkansas 1958. Courtesy of Pat Green

"I don't know whether they'll draft him or not," Colonel Parker interjected. "He's got a nervous condition, you know."

The United States Army disagreed with the Colonel, and in 1957 at the peak of his young career, Elvis got drafted, going from a rock singer's million dollar payroll to Uncle Sam's $78 a

"What about the draft?" the Lubbock reporter asked Elvis at the April show.

"Well, I figure it'll be another six months at least before I get drafted."

A young teen-age girl at his elbows squealed out, "Drafted! Oh, Elvis, you don't mean they're going to draft you."

Presley turned on the grin and said, "I imagine so. After all, I'm just a normal, healthy American boy."

Which brought on more squeals.

Better get used to waiting. Fort Hood 1958. Courtesy of the Fadal Estate

month. On March 24 five hundred crying girls sobbed their good-byes at his induction in Memphis, then followed him to Fort Chaffee, Arkansas. When he emerged from the main building, his trademark pompadour and sideburns filled the dustbin next to the barber's chair. "Hair today, gone tomorrow," he joked with the reporters. The girls renewed their sobs.

After his shots, Elvis received his orders . . . six months in basic training at Fort Hood as one of the Second Armored Division, General George S. Patton's "Hell on Wheels" boys. Elvis bussed to Texas with the other recruits; a convoy of reporters and a sniffle of girls followed. When they arrived at Fort Hood, the tagalongs and the reporters waiting at the base engulfed the new recruit, armed with cameras, Heartbreak Pink lipstick, and notepads. The military police promptly escorted the visitors off the base.

Should he now sign the autographs as Private Presley? Waco 1958. Courtesy of the Fadal Estate

At a press conference. Fort Hood 1958. Courtesy of the Fadal Estate

He and six thousand other soldiers sat in classrooms in the morning and inched along on their bellies through sagebrush and thorny mesquite trees under the broiling afternoon sun. They practiced invasions in the dark, live rounds flying overhead, and hand-to-hand combat with bayonets. They slept with real rattlesnakes. Every day they'd march twenty miles a day over the rolling terrain the Army once used to train American troops against German Panzer tanks in World War II. Elvis did all the tasks the other recruits performed, except that they didn't have carloads of teenagers following them in formation.

Ten hut! Fort Hood 1958.
Courtesy of the Fadal Estate

Cast in the roll as Private Presley, Elvis took to the part with relish. He became just "one of the boys" for the first time in his life. Despite the initial jabs from the other soldiers—"Hey Elvis, where's your hound dog?"—Private Presley woke up every morning to the 5 a.m. reveille just like everyone else.

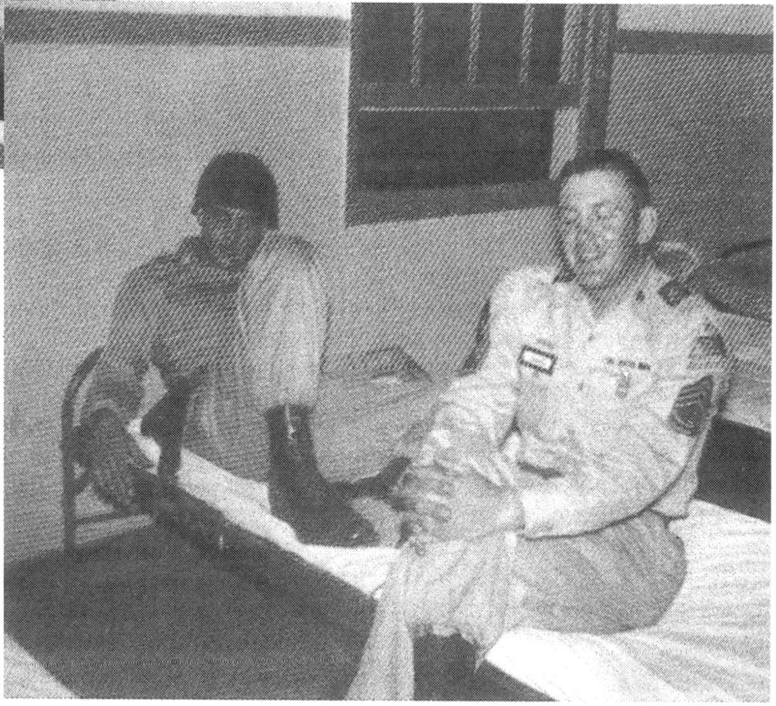

Chillin'. Fort Hood 1958. Courtesy of the Fadal Estate

From the beginning the Army kept his location in the barracks and daily routine a closely guarded secret. Operation Teddy Bear. But Army Intelligence was no match for fan club intelligence. Wherever he marched or stood guard, fans watched him. The locals knew his formation schedule. They lined the roads and sat on their porches and waved. The Army took him off post duty and assigned him to KP, where he peeled potatoes and scrubbed pots and pans like every GI since the beginning of time. He even "bought off" KP duty once for a dollar, a time honored practice in basic training.

So why does he get to wear the armband? Fort Hood 1958. Courtesy of the Fadal Estate

Well howdy there, Private Presley. Fort Hood 1958. Courtesy of the Fadal Estate

The Army grew overly anxious not to show favoritism to their famous recruit. The reporters questioned all aspects of his six-month stay, looking for inconsistencies.

Why did he get to wear green combat leader tabs and the battalion insignia? They asked.

Because he's a squad leader, the Army told them.

If you're lookin' for trouble, well you've come to the right place. Fort Hood 1958. Courtesy of the Fadal Estate

Fort Hood 1958. Courtesy of the Fadal Estate

Gimme a hug, honey. Fort Hood 1958

Aha! And why is he a squad leader?

Because he had prior military experience. He was in the ROTC in high school. It's standard practice.

Sure it is, the reporters retorted in disbelief.

Elvis ignored all criticism and focused on becoming a good soldier, which he surprisingly excelled at (considering the amount of aggressive individualism he displayed before the draft). Elvis surpassed his division in marksmanship and won several Sharpshooter awards with

Reach for the sky. Fort Hood 1958. Courtesy of the Fadal Estate

E. and friend. Fort Hood 1958. Courtesy of the Fadal Estate

Who's the man they call the King?
Who's the man they call the King?
Buys his barracks chicken wings.
Buys his barracks chicken wings.
Sound off.
One, two.
Sound off.
Three, four.
Bring it on down, one, two, three, four.
One, two, three, four.

Fort Hood 1958. Courtesy of the Fadal Estate

After the initial teasing, Elvis and his platoon made peace. During the eight-week barrack restriction, Elvis sprung for fried chicken one night. When the drill sergeant assigned him to drum duty, Elvis added a few extra beats to the cadence to groove up the march. The hip soldiers appreciated his humor and his rhythm.

Occasionally Master Sergeant William Norwood let Elvis sneak off base to meet his girlfriend, Anita Wood. But after basic training, Elvis was given permission to live off base permanently. A trailer manufacturer gave him a promotional trailer for publicity, but he fast outgrew it. Every cousin, second cousin, and even some of the twice removeds of the Presley clan moved in. Eventually Elvis rented a house in the nearby town of Killeen. Elvis begged his parents to come join him and they complied.

In the summer sun, Elvis's dirty blonde hair lightened considerably. Anita Wood and E. at the Fadal home 1958. Courtesy of the Fadal Estate

Every morning he'd arrive at the base in a different colored Lincoln Continental, and return to the full supper table his mother prepared for him. One evening he came home and couldn't hear his mother ask him how his day went. That afternoon the sound of the field artillery had perforated his eardrum. The damage was permanent, and Gladys Presley worried about her son's music career. Elvis played entirely by ear, couldn't even read a note of music. Shortly thereafter, the Army assigned Elvis to the quieter jeep division for the remainder of his training.

For his weekend leaves, Elvis scooted over to the Fadal house in Waco or drove the red and white Lincoln to the Quality Inn in Fort Worth, where he'd girl-watch. The stewardess school in nearby Arlington housed all their

Taking a Hillbilly Catnap. Fort Hood 1958. Courtesy of the Fadal Estate

new interns at the Quality Inn, so the selection was prime.

One July on the way to Fort Worth, a carload of teenagers spotted him. Not wanting the kiddies to cramp his style, Elvis decided to outrun them. He revved the Lincoln to 90 mph and powered over the back roads, the teenagers in hot pursuit. All enjoyed the chase, until a Fort Worth police officer caught them inside the city limits. As the cop pulled both cars over, the kids leaped out of their car and converged on their prey.

"Well, you got me," Elvis told the teens with a laugh. The officer refrained from the general hilarity.

The Pink Room

Like his home in Memphis, the house in Killeen eventually became bombarded by rock 'n' roll pilgrims, drawn from all parts of the United States. Elvis needed another sanctuary, and Gladewater was hours away. Elvis found his new refuge in Waco at the home of his old pal Eddie Fadal.

Elvis and Eddie had met in Dallas a couple of years before when the DJ interviewed him for KRLD radio. Each time Elvis played a concert in Waco, he visited the Fadal house. Eddie often accompanied the singer on the concert tours of '56. When Elvis entered the army, Eddie left an open invitation for him to "come out to the house for a spell and kick your boots off." Elvis took him up on that offer.

Comfortable as an old shoe at the Fadal home, Elvis spent his time jawin' with the home folk, eating, and accompanying little Janice Fadal on the piano while she practiced her scales. Elvis showed up on the weekends and sometimes appeared unexpectedly on their front stoop when he got leave from the base in the middle of the week. Alone or with his friends and cousins, Elvis's arrival always spurred an impromptu family picnic, even if it was only a tablecloth on the floor in front of the television. Hey, *American Bandstand* is on . . . pass the ketchup.

Elvis appeared at their house so often, Eddie built his guest a room, decorated it like Elvis's bedroom in Graceland (the house Elvis bought the previous year), and painted it pink in honor of its grateful recipient.

KRLD Radio 360 presents an interview with Elvis Presley by Eddie Fadal. Courtesy of the Fadal Estate

E. and Eddie Fadal 1958. Courtesy of the Fadal Estate

Nick Adams (left), Eddie Fadal, E., and latest squeeze in Waco 1956. Courtesy of the Fadal Estate

The Fadals decked the room with recording equipment for Elvis to karaoke to his own songs if he liked. The Fadals still have several recordings of him singing "Happy Birthday, Baby" and "Little Darlin" while the kids sang their off-key Jordanaire impression.

One of the toys Elvis played with most, besides his cars, was the custom engineered stereo that ran virtually nonstop in his room. Every week Eddie toted a stack of just-released records home from the radio station. Elvis liked to keep up with who's who and what's what in the music industry during his absence.

At home with the kiddies. Janice, Dana, and E., 1958.
Courtesy of the Fadal Estate

Posing with the movie theater owner and kids. Waco 1958.
Courtesy of James F. Jasek

Darling, Danke Schön

At the end of the summer, rumor began circulating that the platoon would soon get shipped out. A few weeks later the Army confirmed the order. The Second Armored Division would chug out in September by rail.

Where? Where? despairing girls and reporters wanted to know. With sudden keen interest in the Army, the nation's female population urgently looked around to see what bases sat near them, as if Elvis had a choice in the location.

Come to North Carolina, some invited.

Never mind North Carolina. There's a great base out here in Georgia.

How about Florida?

Forget Florida, stay in Texas. Haven't we treated you well?

Germany, the Army announced on the news with finality.

Hasta la vista, baby. Eddie (left of Elvis), E., E's dad Vernon, another cousin, Lamar Fike, and cousin Red West. Waco 1958. Courtesy of the Fadal Estate

GERMANY??!!?? Thousands of devastated females threw themselves on the ground prostrate with grief. No, no, not another country. They won't appreciate him. I heard they don't even speak English.

In Germany confused girls studied the newspaper and stared at the singer's photograph accompanying the story.

Elvis Presley? Wer ist Elvis Presley?

Ich kenne nicht, aber er ist sehr schön.

Ja, ein "hunk."

Colonel Tom Parker slammed the phone down in disgust and anger. Germany. (Unbeknownst to the Presleys or anyone else, Parker was a Dutch illegal alien. If he left the country, even with Elvis on tour, the U.S. wouldn't let him return without a correct passport.)

The Lincoln, like the other cars in the Killeen driveway, were given to charities. The house his parents lived in for the last six months returned from whence it was rented (and resold on eBay a couple of years ago). Elvis left the stereo, recording equipment, and his heart (only figuratively) at the Fadals'.

On September 18 the Fadals threw a bon voyage party for their favorite guest and his acquaintances. All accepted their invitation, and that night the house glowed with family and good friends. They sang and joked and talked about old times, while outside, a quiet crowd gathered on the lawn. Over one hundred well-wishers came to say their goodbyes to the man they'd never met. Elvis looked out a window and saw them. He opened the door and invited the strangers inside. Surprised, they tread hesitantly across the threshold, not wanting to interrupt the party. The front door remained open throughout the evening, and before the night ended, Elvis shook the hand of every soul in the house and danced with all the females, even the children.

The next morning at 2 a.m., hundreds arrived to watch Elvis leave for the depot. He and his platoon would board a train to New York, then ship over to Germany. The base outside of Frankfurt would be his home for the next two years.

Elvis climbed into the car, waved one last time, then just like that, disappeared into the cool pre-dawn darkness.

Good-bye Texas. I'll be back. Courtesy of the Fadal Estate

Epilogue

Despite the worry at the time, Elvis's career didn't end overseas. Reporters kept tabs on him, and his popularity steadily grew in the states like a slow burning flame. When Elvis returned, he found himself more famous than when he left, a feat no other musician can claim.

Elvis made movies, toured, and recorded many of his most famous songs, but he didn't perform in the Lone Star State until the end of his career. Apparently the King felt he'd "done" Texas.

. . . The rest you know.

- 1954 -

October 2, 1954 - Elvis's first and last appearance on the Grand Ole Opry
October 16, 1954 - First Louisiana Hayride appearance
November 21, 1954 - Houston - Magnolia Gardens (afternoon)
November 21, 1954 - Houston - Cook's Hoedown Club (evening)
November 22, 1954 - Gladewater - Mint Club
November 24-27, 1954 - Houston - Paladium Club
December 3, 1954 - Texarkana - Municipal Auditorium
December 17, 1954 - Hawkins - High School Gymnasium
December 1954 - Texarkana - Red River Army Depot at NCO club
December 28, 1954 - Houston - Cook's Hoedown Club Yuletide Jamboree

Two tickets to Paradise.

- 1955 -

January 1, 1955 - Houston - Eagles Hall - Grand Prize Saturday Night Jamboree

January 4, 1955 - Odessa - Senior High School Field House

January 5, 1955 - San Angelo - Municipal City Auditorium

January 6, 1955 - Lubbock - Cotton Club

January 7, 1955 - Midland - High School Auditorium

January 9, 1955 - New Boston High School

January 24, 1955 - Hawkins - Humble Oil Camp

January 25, 1955 - Tyler - Mayfair Building, Fairgrounds

January 26, 1955 - Gilmer - Electric Co-op Administration Building

January 27, 1955 - Longview - Reo Palm Isle Club

January 28, 1955 - Joinerville - Gaston High School Auditorium

February 10, 1955 - Alpine - Alpine High School Auditorium

February 13, 1955 - Lubbock - Fair Park Coliseum (afternoon)

February 13, 1955 - Lubbock - Cotton Club (evening)

February 15, 1955 - Abilene - Fair Park Auditorium

February 16, 1955 - Odessa - Senior High School Field House

February 17, 1955 - San Angelo - Municipal City Auditorium

February 25, 1955 - Texarkana - Municipal Auditorium

March 4, 1955 - DeKalb - High School Gym

March 17, 1955 - Austin - Dessau Hall

March 19, 1955 - College Station - Texas A&M G. Rolle White Coliseum

March 19, 1955 - Houston - Eagles Hall

March 20, 1955 - Houston - Magnolia Gardens (afternoon)

March 20, 1955 - Houston - Cook's Hoedown Club (evening)

March 31, 1955 - Longview - Reo Palm Isle

April 1, 1955 - Odessa - Ector County Auditorium

April 13, 1955 - Breckenridge - High School Auditorium

April 14, 1955 - Gainesville - Owl Park Baseball Field

April 15, 1955 - Stamford - High School (evening)

April 15, 1955 - Stamford - Roundup Hall (late night)

April 16, 1955 - Dallas - Sportatorium

April 21, 1955 - New Boston - High School Football Field

April 22, 1955 - Texarkana - Municipal Auditorium

April 23, 1955 - Waco - Heart O' Texas Coliseum

April 24, 1955 - Houston - Magnolia Gardens (afternoon)

April 24, 1955 - Houston - Cook's Hoedown Club (evening)

April 25, 1955 - Wichita Falls - M-B Corral - (double booked with Seymour)

April 25, 1955 - Seymour - High School Auditorium

April 26, 1955 - Big Spring - Municipal Auditorium

April 28, 1955 - Cisco - Community Hall

April 29, 1955 - Lubbock - Cotton Club

April 30, 1955 - Gladewater - High School Gymnasium

May 20, 1955 - Kilgore - KOCA Radio Baseball Field

May 22, 1955 - Houston - Magnolia Gardens (afternoon)

May 22, 1955 - Houston - Cook's Hoedown Club (evening)

May 27, 1955 - Texarkana - Municipal Auditorium

May 28, 1955 - Dallas - Sportatorium

May 29, 1955 - Fort Worth - North Side Coliseum 4 and 8 p.m.

May 31, 1955 - Midland - High School Auditorium 7:30

May 31, 1955 - Odessa - Senior High School Field House 8:30

June 3, 1955 - Lubbock - Johnson-Connelly Pontiac 7 p.m.

June 3, 1955 - Lubbock - Fair Park Coliseum 8 p.m.

June 8, 1955 - Sweetwater - Municipal Auditorium

June 9, 1955 - Andrews - High School

June 10, 1955 - Breckenridge - American Legion Hall

June 16, 1955 - Texarkana - Municipal Auditorium

June 17, 1955 - Stamford - High School (evening)

June 17, 1955 - Stamford - Roundup Hall (late night)

June 18, 1955 - Dallas - Sportatorium

June 19, 1955 - Houston - Magnolia Gardens (afternoon)

June 19, 1955 - Houston - Cook's Hoedown Club (evening)

June 20-21, 1955 - Beaumont - Municipal Auditorium

July 3, 1955 - Corpus Christi - Hoedown Club

July 4, 1955 - Stephenville - Recreation Hall (morning)

July 4, 1955 - DeLeon - Hodges Park (afternoon)

July 4, 1955 - Brownwood - Soldiers-Sailors Municipal Auditorium (evening)

July 23, 1955 - Dallas - Big D Jamboree

August 7, 1955 - Houston - Magnolia Gardens (afternoon)

August 7, 1955 - Houston - Cook's Hoedown Club (evening)

August 8, 1955 - Tyler - Mayfair Building Fairgrounds

August 9, 1955 - Henderson - Rodeo Arena

August 10, 1955 - Gladewater - Baseball Field

August 11, 1955 - Longview - Reo Palm Isle

August 12, 1955 - Kilgore - Driller Baseball Field

August 22, 1955 - Wichita Falls - Spudder Baseball Field

August 23, 1955 - Bryan - Saddle Club on Rodeo Grounds

August 24, 1955 - Conroe - High School Football Field

August 25, 1955 - Austin - Sport Center

August 26, 1955 - Gonzales - Baseball Field

September 2, 1955 - Texarkana - Municipal Auditorium

September 3, 1955 - Dallas - Sportatorium

September 3, 1955 - Dallas - Roundup Club (late night)

September 26, 1955 - Gilmer - High School Auditorium

October 3, 1955 - College Station - Texas A&M G. Rolle White Coliseum

October 4, 1955 - Paris - Boys Club Gym Auditorium

October 5, 1955 - Greenville - Municipal Auditorium

October 6, 1955 - San Marcos - Southwest Texas State University

October 6, 1955 - Austin - Skyline Club

October 8, 1955 - Houston - City Auditorium

October 9, 1955 - Cherry Springs - Cherry Springs Dance Hall

October 10, 1955 - Brownwood - Soldiers-Sailors Memorial Hall

October 11, 1955 - Abilene - Fair Park Auditorium

October 12, 1955 - Midland - High School Auditorium

October 13, 1955 - Amarillo - Municipal Auditorium

October 14, 1955 - Odessa - Senior High School Field House

October 15, 1955 - Lubbock - Fair Park Coliseum

October 15, 1955 - Lubbock - Cotton Club (evening)

November 12, 1955 - Carthage - Texas Mill Company Opening

November 17, 1955 - Texarkana - Municipal Auditorium

November 18, 1955 - Longview - Reo Palm Isle Club

November 19, 1955 - Gladewater - High School Gymnasium

November 25, 1955 - Port Arthur - Woodrow Wilson High School Auditorium

- 1956 -

January 15, 1956 - San Antonio - Municipal Auditorium

January 16, 1956 - Galveston - Municipal Auditorium

January 17, 1956 - Beaumont - Municipal Auditorium

January 18, 1956 - Austin - Austin Coliseum

January 19, 1956 - Wichita Falls - Memorial Auditorium

January 20, 1956 - Fort Worth - North Side Coliseum

April 9, 1956 - Wichita Falls - Memorial Auditorium

April 10, 1956 - Lubbock - Fair Park Coliseum

April 11, 1956 - El Paso - El Paso Coliseum

April 13, 1956 - Amarillo - Municipal Auditorium

April 15, 1956 - San Antonio - Municipal Auditorium

April 16, 1956 - Corpus Christi - Memorial Coliseum

April 17, 1956 - Waco - Heart O' Texas Coliseum

April 20, 1956 - Fort Worth - North Side Coliseum

April 21, 1956 - Houston - City Auditorium

October 11, 1956 - Dallas - Cotton Bowl, Texas State Fair

October 12, 1956 - Waco - Heart O' Texas Coliseum

October 13, 1956 - Houston - Sam Houston Coliseum

October 14, 1956 - San Antonio - Bexar County Coliseum

We'd like to thank the following folks for allowing us to surf their neural highways (as well as borrow their pictures). Y'all are the most!

Lois Adair
Shirley Stewart
Willie Cox
Elsie Medlin
I.G. Holmes
Sid Foster
Doug Dixon
Karolee Flennigan
Carolyn Bradshaw
Tillman Franks
Billie Garrett
Pat Cupp
Jane Hopkins
Cheesie Nelson
Billy Bob Pruitt
Rob Lowe Jr.
Wallace Reed
Hal Long
David Denard
Weldene Robinson
Jay Thompson
Steve Bonner
Alice Reese
Bill Mack
Johnny Stokes
Polly Crawford Webb
Jesse Winchester
Tony Ventura
Kay Wheeler
Pat Green
Sherry Davis
Judy Metz Jackson
Marileon Hopkins Jerden
Jo McGill
Janice and Dana Fadal
Traci Nelson Dockery
Jimmy Willis
James F. Jasek
Carol Lloyd

If you saw Elvis in Texas, we'd love to hear your story. E-mail us at ElvisInTexas@yahoo.com

In fond memory
of
Smokey Montgomery
1913-2001
and
Dr. Carl "Cheesie" Nelson
1939-2001

Index